ABUNDANCE
ENLIGHTENMENT

*An Easy Motivational Guide to
the Laws of Attracting in Abundance
and Transforming Your Soul*

KEVIN HUNTER

WARRIOR
OF LIGHT
PRESS

Warrior of Light Press
www.kevin-hunter.com

Body, Mind & Spirit/Spiritualism
Body, Mind & Spirit/New Thought
Self-Help/Motivational & Inspirational

Some of the content in this book was featured in the book, "*Living for the Weekend*", along with additional brand new material.

WARRIOR OF LIGHT
POCKET BOOK SERIES

Spirit Guides and Angels
Soul Mates and Twin Flames
Raising Your Vibration
Divine Messages for Humanity
Connecting with the Archangels
The Seven Deadly Sins
Love Party of One
A Beginner's Guide to the Four Psychic Clair Senses
Twin Flame Soul Connections
Attracting in Abundance
Abundance Enlightenment

♥

Available in Paperbook and E-Book:
ATTRACTING IN ABUNDANCE

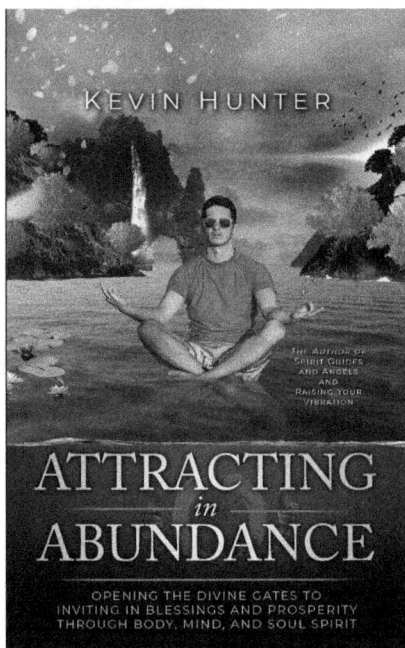

Contents

AUTHOR NOTE

Abundance Enlightenment is the follow up book to the abundance guide available called *Attracting in Abundance*. Some of the content in this book was featured in the book, *Living for the Weekend*. The reason the content surrounding the law of attracting in abundance is available on its own here with additional content is that there are readers that won't be interested in the *Living for the Weekend* book. Some of the abundance related content in that book was important enough to make available for those just interested in that particular material, as I wanted others to have access to it.

My books are typically infused with practical messages and divine guidance from myself and my Spirit team. We share this with readers interested or guided to the material. The main goal is to fine-tune your body, mind, and soul. You are a Divine communicator capable of receiving messages and guidance from Heaven, as all souls are.

My Spirit team makes up God and the Holy Spirit, as well as a team of guides, angels, and sometimes Archangels and Saints. I am merely the liaison or messenger in delivering and interpreting the intentions of what they wish to communicate.

My team includes some hard truth telling Wise Ones from the other side, including Saint Nathaniel, who can be brutal in his direct forcefulness. He cuts right to the heart of humanity without apology. I have learned quite a bit from him while adopting his ideology, which is Heaven's philosophy as a whole.

If I use the word "He" when pertaining to God, this does not mean that I am advocating that he is a male. Simply replace the word, "He" with one you are comfortable using to identify God for you to be. If the word, "God" makes you uncomfortable, then substitute it with one you're more familiar with. This goes for any gender I use as examples. When I say, "spirit team", I am referring to a team of 'Guides and Angels'.

One of the purposes of my work is to empower, enlighten, as well as entertain. It's to help improve aspects of yourself that you long to work on, as well as your soul, your life, and humanity by default. It does not matter if you are a beginner or well versed in the subject matter. There may be content that reminds you of what you already know or something that you were unaware of. We all have much to share with one another, as we are all one in the end.

~ Kevin Hunter

ABUNDANCE
ENLIGHTENMENT

CHAPTER ONE

Working with the Law of Attraction

Ultimate authentic success surrounds your soul's growth and evolving process. It's when you realize that none of the physical ego driven desires matter in the end. You can work hard to make sure you stay afloat, you're able to pay your bills, and support yourself and family, but you're not chasing friends, likes, followers, fans, or people to prop you up. Any amount of goodness displayed from your heart is the true measure of real accomplishment.

An overflowing feeling of optimism and love coupled with faith and action is what increases the chances of attracting good things and positive experiences to you.

Believing you can be anything you want to be is an exceptional perspective to help you thrive and persevere forward. Give yourself a grand shot at achieving what you agreed to this lifetime by putting in daily or weekly action steps required to make what you dream of become a reality. It is not a far-fetched notion to trust you can and will conquer your dreams as other countless successes throughout history have. They started out with nothing, but a dream and persisted forward to make what they longed for become a reality. They ignored the naysayers or dream crushers, wiped that out of their minds, and forged forward under the power of God and the Universe. It is better to believe in yourself and what you are capable of than to not believe.

Be an unswerving fighter, have passion, persistence, drive, and a strong will to succeed in all you desire and long to accomplish. That's been my long running secret to achieve what I've done to date. I'm often approached by others informing me how my accomplishments, history, and unshakeable work ethic has inspired them. My life, temperament, regimen, and process is similar to that of an Olympic athlete that it's exhausted some around me. I have to be prepared on all levels through body, mind, and soul to give 110%, otherwise I won't bother to commit to it. If I'm committed to something, then I can't be stopped.

The steps towards making your dreams come true are simple: Believe you can do it with great upbeat enthusiastic optimism that rarely wavers. Increase your faith in a higher power by allowing that essence to fill you up each morning you wake up propelling you to seize the day. Ask for help from God and your Spirit team through prayer. Pay attention to the guidance they give you and take action on it. The guidance might not come the second you make the request, but stay alert and pay attention to the signs you see throughout your day that could be their answer. If you're getting the nudge to exercise more, then follow that guidance. They know that when you take care of all parts of you that this contributes to your overall soul success, which equates to abundance success.

Your Spirit team is made up of one guardian angel and one spirit guide. Someone may have more than one guide and one angel if they regularly work with beings in Heaven. If a person has more challenging goals and purposes they need to accomplish while here, then they may also have more than one guide and angel. This might be that person attempting to make grander changes for the benefit of humanity. They may not even be aware that there is a Spirit team available around to help them. No one is exempt from heavenly help, including non-believers of a higher power, which is why they reach success by believing they can.

For some people, there are more guides and angels sifting in and out if that person requires more. This could be the case if you have major goals needed to accomplish that are beneficial for your higher self's purpose. For instance, inventors throughout history would have had more than one guide or angel working with them through the process of their inventing from the idea and on down to the finished product. This is to help bring great inventions to people such as electricity, running water, materials to build homes, etc. The guides specializing in that would stay throughout that tenure whether it's months or years. There is no time restricted limit. They stay for as long as needed, then they move onto assist others once the goal was fulfilled.

Your Spirit team is assigned to you before you are born into a human life. You also know them while you are a soul before you incarnate into a human birth. You've met with them and discussed some of the purposes you intend to accomplish on Earth before your arrival. They are present at your birth and remain with you through human death.

Some guides and angels might agree to show up at a certain juncture of someone's life, such as when major life changes are taking place. They leave once it's calmed down and heavenly help is no longer needed for that circumstance. A spirit guide may be sent to you to assist in preparing you for a particular love relationship partner, or to help you find a specific job where you will learn valuable lessons and skills at in order to utilize later in your personal and/or professional life. Once you and this love partner have connected, or you obtained the job you desired, then that particular guide will leave.

Your one main spirit guide and one guardian

angel will never leave your side no matter what. They are your day-to-day team ready and alert should their assistance be needed. They act as God's hands and arms ensuring you stay on path. They are some of the souls you stand face to face with upon your arrival at Heaven's gate upon human death. This is also when all of the answers to questions you had throughout your Earthly life that were never answered flow through you with exceptional clarity. It will feel like you had been carrying those answers around with you all that time, but it wasn't strong enough to be picked up on. This will change as you cross over into the bliss filled Heavenly realms where your soul originated.

Your Spirit team's primary role is to guide you along your Earthly journey ensuring that both the blessings and challenges you're intended to encounter take place. You also have free will choice to either tune into their guidance and follow it, or ignore it and venture off on your own path. The latter can cause problems since that is often times the ego's choice. The ego is only interested in holding you back or getting you into trouble. Some consider the ego to be the Darkness or the Devil, which are all interchangeable the same way God can mean the Universe, the Light, Spirit, or a Higher Power to different people depending on who you talk to. It's all the same thing regardless of the label human beings choose to call it.

Your Spirit team can warn you against making a particular choice if they see you are heading towards danger, but they cannot always stop you from that. This is especially the case if you're brushing off divine spirit guidance and ignoring it. How often throughout your life has an undesirable circumstance taken place that prompts you to later realize you had actually been warned? I know I've certainly heard others say, "And I knew I shouldn't have done that. I had this really strong nudge not to do that, but I just ignored it."

Some people have made poor choices out of being deeply in love with someone. Heaven applauds love feelings for another person, but they know the side effect to intense obsessive love could fog up your psychic vision and divine connection. This can contribute to you making choices you might not have ordinarily done if those rose-colored glasses weren't tightly on. Some people have been in a love situation where they were in love with someone who wasn't as in love with them back. This continues until they find out they were being taken advantage of by that partner. They look back and start to recall the many red flags and Divine signs offered to them about this new prospect. Those signs had been in front of them all along, but because they were in the deep blinding haze of being in this kind of love attraction they failed to notice it or brushed it off.

When you're that in love with someone you let them get away with murder, until they react cruelly to you in a way that snaps you back to reality. You realize you knew all along they were wrong for you, but you had been deceived by the dark ego.

Those strong feeling sense nudges you get can be your ego, or it can be coming from a member or members of your Spirit team trying to communicate with you in warning. As you grow more in tune with your soul and the Divine, you get better at differentiating what is your ego and what is your Spirit team. Since Spirit cannot pick up the phone and call you, or write you an email, they use other methods to communicate with you that work. These methods include communicating with you through your etheric senses that include Clairvoyance, Clairsentience, Claircognizance, and Clairaudience. I discuss the four clairs in greater detail in my book, *Four Clair Psychic Senses*, since it would be too long for this particular piece.

Your Spirit team will guide and assist you where it's possible within their means of being able to do so, but it is up to you to pull yourself up and stand tall no matter how tough life can be. Lean on them for support, stay strong in faith, have gratitude, and ask for repetitive daily assistance. They can help guide you on your path towards abundance enlightenment. Pay attention to the signs in your path that require you to act towards this positive change, then take those action steps to get the energy moving in the direction of your dreams.

ABUNDANCE ENLIGHTENMENT

Chasing monetary success can leave you dissatisfied. Monetary success isn't long lasting, but spiritual success is. There's nothing corrupt about being adequately paid for your hard work, otherwise you risk being taken advantage. This can happen if you give away your time and services for free. This isn't about helping those in need for free, which counts in the giving and receiving equation. This can be about your job or career. If for example you're trying to physically survive, but offer free readings and consultations to those that reach out to you, then that would apply here.

This is a physical world that requires money to survive on this planet. It's misguided to believe that money isn't everything. It is true that money is not everything compared to love, great health, and good loyal friends that understand you and have your back, but the reality is that money is required to survive on the planet. Find that steady balance where you gracefully thrive to achieve to make enough money to be comfortable enough where you no longer have worry of not being able to pay your bills. At the same time, avoid getting too carried away with it that you fall into greed territory, which is an abundance killer.

Abundance is more than monetary and financial increase. It can also be about reaching an awe-inspiring optimistic heavenly well-being state of joy, peace, and love. This positive emotional mindful state simultaneously attracts in blessings.

It is the basic human necessities that people tend to chase after over anything else. Some continue chasing these things long after they have it due to a greed mentality or because they are looking to fill up a missing void inside. They may not even realize this as being the reason for chasing. Having a lack of spiritual awareness to all things beyond the physical can increase a desire to chase after external physical material gratification to fill that emptiness. The end result propels you to constantly search for these physical material gratifications that end up leaving you empty after you've obtained it. Strike a healthy balance between having one foot grounded into physical reality and another foot in the spirit etheric planes outside of physical reality. This is that sweet spot where an overwhelming positive feeling of abundance rises and increases.

It is not immoral to desire to live securely enough where you have a comfortable place to live, a career, job, and/or hobbies that fulfill you. Your bills get paid without worry and you have a love partner or a healthy social circle. When you're taken care of with your physical needs, then it is easier to focus on what others need. When you feel safe and secure, then your vibration is raised within that comfy nest. This makes you a joy to be around and a powerful abundance magnet at the same time.

Your emotional and mental well-being state is important for numerous reasons. When you're happy and healthy, then the more love and abundance you attract in. This also raises your vibration, which awakens your intuitive psychic connection with Spirit. It is that connection which helps you receive divinely guided information and inspiration designed to keep you on the right path towards soul enlightenment and beyond.

Enlightenment is that content space your soul secretly seeks deep down. It is the place you resided in when you were born, but Earthly life circumstances dulled that beautiful edge that exists within the core of your soul. If you have the hope of brightening it up again, then I know how you feel, as I've been in that place in the past myself. I did whatever I could to get that emotional and mental state unnaturally, which entailed getting my hands on any toxic addiction possible. I wound up running around in circles chasing a mirage. Only when I tuned back in to my Spirit team was I able to manage life more efficiently.

In the past, when I have been on cloud nine, that was when I saw positive circumstances filter in. When I was down or negative, then either more of that came into my life, or nothing changed at all. To an extent, having positive thoughts and an optimistic mindset will work, but this needs to be backed up with faith and action. It's certainly better than being bitter, angry, and negative. Which person would you like to hang out with? I'm going to go with the happy loving camper who just wants to have a good time and wants you to have one too.

CHAPTER TWO

Attract in Abundant Success

*T*he law of attraction is an interesting principle because on the one hand being positive all day will not automatically equate to positive things falling on your doorstep. It will definitely contribute to the success of attracting in abundance over having a negative disposition. Someone might have a general happy disposition, but they forever struggle in the practical world unable to obtain that lucky break that changes their life for the better. I've witnessed others put on the false positive façade to people, but deep down they were battling to the point they were resorting to getting ahead through deceptive means. This only pushed their ultimate goal and destination further away, and sometimes brought upon their downfall.

You might have noticed that a miserable curmudgeon seems to rise up the ranks in the business world attracting bountiful finances to purchase their three mansions, two yachts, and a hot Ferrari. This is because the laws of attraction are not a cut and dry method of obtaining what you desire. Each person is a separate study to determine what their overall disposition is, and then you weigh that against their achievements, desires, and accomplishments. With that said, having optimism far supersedes being indefinitely pessimistic.

A business executive might be an angry killjoy, but it is unlikely that they are pessimistic. Pessimism does not help anyone with obtaining and achieving much. When you fall into perpetual pessimism, then the greater the chances that you will witness one challenging circumstance after another happening in your life. This is one side of what can cause a challenging circumstance to take place. The other side is based on your free will choices that will put that into motion. Your soul does not grow and evolve as much when everything is going swimmingly for it. You need challenges to shape, mold, and improve your soul's growth.

Optimism can and will help attracting good things into your life more swiftly than not. This is because optimism is one of a handful of ingredients to add to what is a recipe for success. Miserable people who have achieved may obtain what they desire, but if one compares that to any personal issues they end up battling with, then the cons may far offset the pros. They can end up battling rapidly failing health, to the loss or absence of a good love partner and loyal friendships, to witnessing their own downfall. This has been seen on countless occasions with public figures in the media.

The law of attraction works to an extent, but one of the numerous factors to take into account is that those who are doing their best to attract what they want may unknowingly stall or reverse the process. This is by vacillating in your mind between knowing you will get what you want, to experiencing fear or doubts that it will never happen. The second you experience fears, worries, or doubts, then you negate the positive attraction movement. The effects are reversed back in the other direction. This is why it sometimes feels as if you're taking two steps forward and one step back.

It is highly rare to see someone who is in a perpetual depression state receive consistent blessings. Being in a permanent depressed state cripples you from working hard and taking action steps. One action step the depressed person takes is seen with no return. The depressed person gives up and retreats for awhile longer than necessary. This stalls the positive attracting energy movement that was initiated by the one action step originally taken. It now moves back down in the other direction creating a block to abundance, until there is consistent action being taken to bring it back towards opening the abundance gate. Keeping the action momentum going is what helps in getting that abundant fire started.

It is unusual that someone who is continuously angry will receive overflowing blessings. This angry person can be working hard in a rage trying to create some kind of dent that never takes off, thus making them more angry and stressed. It's that stress filled anger that drops the vibration energy and simultaneously blocks abundance. They will forever be fighting against the wind until that demeanor is shifted and dominated by a more optimistic mindset and detachment to their desired outcome. The journey is more important than the destination. It is the journey where you are making lifestyle adjustments to make you more of a positive abundance attractor, because this isn't something that happens over night. You are adjusting your soul frequency through time to move into alignment.

When you reach your goal and destination, you could wind up asking the question, "Now what?" An ambitious soul whose goal is to forever evolve and grow will always ask that question no matter how many hooves they have planted into the ground.

You have to believe you will obtain what you desire more than believing you will not. 60% of the time or more you need to believe that you will obtain your desire. It would need to be more optimism than pessimism. When you drop below the 50% mark, say 20% optimism and 80% pessimism, then that is not enough gas to get your car moving far enough to reach the success destination. The optimism quotient needs to be what dominates most of the time.

It's okay to fall into pessimism or doubt once in a while, but it's so miniscule that it barely cripples or inhibits your forward movement towards abundance enlightenment. It flushes in and out quick enough that you stand back up like a warrior ready to forge forward with optimism. You don't allow the pessimism to hold you down preventing you from movement.

Achieving success is more than believing you will achieve your dreams with optimism. It is also incorporating faith coupled with action. Those are the other two essential ingredients to add to the mix. It is not enough to believe you will get something by doing nothing. This is how those seemingly mean people achieve their desires. They believe they will get it and they take action to make it happen. They may be miserable people, but they believe they will get what they want, and as a result they achieve success.

Saying that someone is miserable is subjective. They might appear that way, when in fact they are as happy as can be to those close to them. They are just ambitious, which to some is considered a dirty word that has the stigma of something negative to some folks. Ambition is not a dirty word when it comes to productivity and creativity. This is someone who loves what they do and they keep doing it with a great attitude, hence they start to see blessings coming in because of that. Successful people or those longing for success in achieving their goals will see ambition as a positive word.

When looking to attract in something you desire,

avoid thinking about or entertaining anything associated with fear. This is fear that what you want won't happen or fear that you're not qualified for something. Fear is a dangerous emotion that is conjured up by the human ego. It produces incredible uproar and upset individually and globally. If you want something, then go out and get it without skepticism or hesitation.

When something positive or good is offered to a pessimist, the pessimist will reply with something negative. Having that point of view and mindset is a block guaranteeing that it will never happen.

An optimistic person says, "I'll figure out a way to do it."

While a negative person says, "That's easier said than done."

Notice the difference in those opposing statements. The first person will end up achieving successful results, while the second person will remain stagnant and stuck until they change their attitude and put some fight into their life.

If you find your response to something positive is countered with something negative, then work on being aware of that, then shift it into something positive immediately. I have watched many people reside in negativity and nothing good ever happens for them. I've seen people that have a positive mindset receive good things constantly flowing towards them, around them, and into their life. This has been evident in the data, statistics, and stories available to notice the pattern.

Who said getting what you want was going to be easy? You need to have passion, be a fighter and a shark to get what you want. When I wanted something, I went after it and I eventually got it. I had zero fear, training, experience, time, money, and support, but I defied those roadblocks and went after it fearlessly anyway. The end result was that I succeeded.

Hone in on what you want and work harder than anyone you've come across, until you attain your desires, but then keep going. Pull yourself up by your bootstraps and do your best to work hard to get what you want. This method can be applied to work related endeavors or your friendships and love relationships.

Incorporate regular sessions of break time, retreats, quiet time, and personal time, so that you don't burn out. The burn out feeling can also slow down the attraction business. This is why taking those day or weekend trips to somewhere in nature can help get your soul re-calibrated and re-aligned. It's a healthy way to re-charge your batteries.

This personal time is a much needed intermission your soul needs regular amounts of. This is how you participate in self-love and self-care. It is time devoted to you alone or with a loved one. When you're alone sitting in a park, in meditation, or in nature somewhere, you're able to clear your mind and allow perspective and additional Divinely guided ideas to flow into your soul without any physical distractions. You gather up the newly gained incoming ammunition and tools and store it away for future use. When you re-emerge from your personal time and back into the next phase of your action momentum, you apply what you've learned into this new chapter of forward motion. Take your time and enjoy what you're doing as you move one action step closer towards your goals, dreams, and destination.

Nothing was ever handed to me throughout my life without working for it. Growing up I'd watch others obtain things seemingly effortlessly while I struggled. I knew I had to work for what I wanted or it would never transpire. If I entertained that rare doubt, then what I was focusing on wouldn't happen, or a whirlwind of negative circumstances and delays popped up. This is another hypothesis I've tested out throughout my life to ensure it works for me first. I'm unable to stand behind anything I'm not experienced with firsthand. Wise Ones will be naturally skeptical about anything and everything until they've immersed themselves into it wholly to determine whether it's something worth taking on and adopting or not.

You may have dreams you desire to bring to fruition, but the dream feels far away, unobtainable, and overwhelming that it leaves you wondering how you're ever going to make it happen. You end up not bothering with it and falling into procrastination techniques that continue to delay any movement from being seen. Before you know it, several years have flown by. You wake up and look back on those years wondering where they went. You wonder what you had been doing that whole time, because you're nowhere near achieving that bliss you forever longed for. There's no way you should agree to live like that. You don't want to live like a sitting duck waiting to die. Instead, at least try and put some fight into it.

I've been plagued by social anxiety and social phobias my entire life, but when I wanted something deeply, I refused to let that stop me. I walked in with those anxieties, and nailed what I wanted with those fears in there. It's kind of like some entertainers before they take the stage to face a stadium full of people. They admitted to being nervous beforehand no matter how good or experienced they are at performing. They sucked it up and went out there to do the job they agreed to do. Once they were deep in that particular job, they noticed the free flowing momentum that took place. It became suddenly effortless and second nature to them.

The Universe and your Spirit team are not going to hand you anything for free. They help those that help themselves. They open doors for those they see are doing their best to put in an effort, regardless if that person is a believer in a higher power or not. This is why you have likely heard or witnessed atheists or non-believers achieve great things. It's because they believed they could do it, so they went after it with enormous passion and achieved it. They are not exempt from success because they're not believers of a higher power. A higher power or spirit beings have no judgment on such things. If they see someone trying to achieve something great, then they will lend them an additional hand regardless of believing in spirit or not.

The main ingredients to add to the recipe to

attract in abundant success are simple to remember because it's not a long list. The following requires consistent regular momentum to crack open the doors to abundance:

· Optimism and Enthusiasm

· Faith and Prayer

· Action

CHAPTER THREE

Abundance, Money, and Productivity

*E*very soul's life moves up and down through a series of chapters within that one lifetime. Some chapters are more challenging with numerous roadblocks than others, while other chapters are filled with bright blessings. Each chapter tells a different story for each person in their life's book. When you begin each chapter of your life, you are giving birth to a brand new start with a clean slate that should be accompanied with a fresh optimism and outlook, which are essential ingredients to manifesting abundance.

Abundance is a word that gets flown around predominately in spiritual and religious circles, even though most people are aware of what that word means. This has made the genre somewhat intoxicating because everyone wants to live a life full of abundance, even if they don't use that word. Abundance sounds attractive to the ego, which desires all the material riches that life has to offer. A guru uses the abundance word, and others grow interested and enticed because you feel you're in a position where abundance doesn't seem to be present.

People want and desire things that will make them feel comfortable. Everyone is attracted to money and finances for the benefits and the luxuries that it can offer and assist with. This is a physical world and like it or not, spiritual or not, it takes money to make certain things happen. Abundance is not always financial and can be about experiencing positive emotional well-being traits such as happiness, fruitful friends, good relationships, great health, and an evolving joyful spiritual nature. All of those elements help crack open the abundance door even more.

Many understandably require money to be able survive, rent an apartment without worry of running out of money that you can no longer afford it. It can be to purchase a home of your dreams, food, clothing, and all of the necessities that help you live comfortably enough that money is no longer a worry filled desire. Money enables you to be able to focus on your life purpose work that may entail helping others in some way. God knows that when you don't worry about money and no longer need to take up a job you don't care about, that it can free you to put all of that extra energy towards your life purpose.

On the flipside, money has been the instigator of people seeking power, suing for money, stealing money, breaking into cars and homes, and even killing over money. Money drives people towards making dangerously greedy choices and behavior patterns. This leads them to lie, steal, and cheat their way towards obtaining money through deceptive means. All of this creates inevitable bad karma where that person ends up having to pay it back in some form at some point in their life whether immediately or down the line. Eventually your luck runs out if you've been trying to obtain through deceptive means. Because that behavior is so potent, the karma is multiplied to the point they end up having to pay for it indefinitely.

If this wasn't a planet that required finances to physically survive, then one wouldn't need to worry about slumming it at a job they don't care about it in order to stay afloat. Earthly life is physical world that requires money as the sole source of survival. This is the case even if money has no value or validity when you pass on. Until then you need to make an adequate amount of money to survive. You don't need to be a money hungry business person whose main goal is to keep finding ways to make more money long after you've achieved beyond your means. Collecting money for the sake of it isn't a goal to thrive for that enhances your soul's growth.

If there is any positive benefit to having the goal of making money it's for the positive uses that one does with it that can help others. For example, this would apply to a rich business investor that constantly seeks to make more money, but uses that money to give jobs to those who need it, or to those that can be lifted out of poverty. In that respect, the money seeking business person is using the money for good. It is to keep staff employed, which in turn helps their physical survival. There are great many people who have made those millions and are comfortable enough with much more to give that they find ways to help others lives with it. In that respect, it would have a positive benefit. Collecting money to ensure your long term retirement in senior age is ensuring your security is in place, which is having a positive benefit as well too. The chasing money due to an obsession over money even though you're set for life would fall into a negative reason for achieving money.

JUDGING APPEARANCES

Judging someone based on appearance creates an abundance block. It's the negative energy that is associated with the act of judging that prevents the positive flow of abundance. For example, some have called the rich and wealthy derogatory terms, but not all rich people have that appearance about them. Many successful financially well off people don't always appear rich or snobby. They could be that guy with the jeans, t-shirt, and flip-flops. The look that gives the illusion of a slacker, but then you find out he's the multi-millionaire genius that created a successful startup company. There are wealthy folks accustomed to a certain lifestyle. They merged into that personality where they could purchase whatever they want for however much they want. Imagine having all the money in the world and how that might alter your personality to a degree.

I've run social experiment tests where I've walked into a place looking run down in the t-shirt, flip-flops, and jeans attire and I've been treated with disinterest. On another day, I will dress to the riches and walk into the same place and suddenly they're all smiles and bowing down. My eyes are secretly narrowing with that internal eye roll knowing they don't realize that I'm the same person they dismissed the other day, but now I'm so dressed up to the point of being unrecognizable from that other guy.

That scenario is actually kind of like that scene in the film, *Pretty Woman,* where she's initially judged and treated horribly by the sales women because of her appearance. When she walks into the store at a later date dressed to the nines they are suddenly catering to her, all smiles, and sucking up. She illuminates them that she was the same woman from before and won't be giving them her business. The sales people look stunned not realizing it was the same person. The human ego resides on a shallow level judging a person by their appearance, which as the film pointed out is a huge mistake.

We also saw this set up in *Beauty and the Beast*, where an arrogant Prince turns an ugly old woman beggar away because of how she looks. When the old woman transforms into a beautiful stunning woman enchantress, he suddenly pleads to be forgiven, but it was too late. The enchantress casts a spell turning him into a hideous monstrous Beast in order for him to learn something valuable. He'll have to learn to work extra hard to get people to like him because of how he looks. Sadly people are superficial and judge you on how you look, instead of what is in your heart. This is a tale as old as time on Earth.

All these centuries into evolution, and not much progression has been made on this planet surrounding that. People are still judging others by how they appear and what they have while pretending to fight and care for the underdog. You witness how judgmental and dismissive of you someone is until they see someone good looking. They suddenly bow down to the hot good looking person, even if the good looking person has no deep soul essence. Now you've fallen into superficial primitiveness. The arrogant ego treats others that are not attractive to them with disrespect.

FIGHT TO ATTRACT IN ABUNDANCE

It is often said that money is the root of evil, but that's because in some circles you're also taught to see money as bad or dirty. When you view money that way, then you create a block from obtaining it. This doesn't mean you're intended to glorify money, but it does mean to accept the reality that money is needed to survive on the planet. Otherwise millions of people all over the world wouldn't remain in jobs that have become unfulfilling to them. Those jobs have become more like a lifelong prison sentence with a coffin waiting in the wings for you to climb into and accept the ultimate fate.

You could be someone that struggles to make ends meet in a job you don't care for. No matter how hard you try to create a dent to improve matters, not much change happens to improve your life, while others experience a domino effect of hard times. No one is exempt from challenges on some level. It's true it can appear that others seem to have it easier, but if you don't know them personally, then you're likely unaware of what they're battling with behind closed doors. I've never come across someone who was on cloud nine every single minute of every day.

Some people are born with a genetic predisposition to being happy in general. For others, that happy feeling seems to come onto them once they've achieved some measure of physical life satisfaction. This can be such as getting the guy or girl for a romantic relationship, to getting that great job, or achieving a financial breakthrough in your career, to buying that first house, or receiving a big financial check. It's much easier to naturally move your well-being state into a feeling of happiness only after you receive some kind of good news. Fighting to get happy without your desires coming to fruition becomes a fight for so many people.

It's easy for a popular financially successful guru teacher to preach about optimism and positive thoughts when they already have the home, great career, friends, and love relationship. It's not challenging to have those things and then lecture others with lesser means on getting happy.

I may be an optimist, but I'm also a practical realist. The discord between pessimism and optimism is not as wide when you have those physical material things already in your life. Moving your vibration into the zone of happiness takes more effort. Still there are people who have all of the material comforts most people desire, but are permanently unhappy and unfulfilled, because true happiness starts from within. If you were miserable before money, you may be miserable after obtaining money. One of the top easiest steps towards bringing in abundance is getting happy first, then the rest will follow.

Partaking in what you love today without the money has a greater chance of bringing in the money later. Examine many of the popular entertainers in history that were not looking to get into their craft for the money. They just wanted to be an entertainer. The money came in later, but it wasn't the goal or ultimate interest.

My social circle is in all economic brackets from the working class to the rich and famous. Every single one of them is battling at least one challenging thing in their day-to-day life. Having financial riches isn't going to make other problems go away. Money can help to the degree that you're no longer worrying about having money to survive. That is a definite reality that can't be twisted or written off.

You're able to divert your focus towards your life purpose and passions when you have enough income filtering into your life that you can live worry free. This worry free is the absence of concern that your bills won't get paid. Having millions of dollars will not ensure that other areas of your life won't have worry. The positive benefit to having enough of an income with your life purpose hobby passion work is that you no longer have to slug it in a job you don't care for. This is that job where you put on the fake smile that all is well, when deep down your Spirit team knows how you really feel about it. They want to help move you out of that since high vibrational spirit beings do not desire to see someone suffer.

In my early twenties, I was living check to check or I was struggling to find a job. Eventually after much fight and perseverance, I started finding great work, and was making more than enough money to live comfortably without worry, but then there were other issues that would arise. Life is full of issues beyond money that pop up from interpersonal connections, to physical, mental, and/or emotional health issues, to the day to day operations of the practical part of your life. This is also seen with well-known artists who have the millions, but admit to some kind of mental health issue they're battling with. Others scoff or state they have a hard time feeling sorry for them when they have all that money in their bank account. As if money will get rid of a negative mental health state. If you were battling mental health issues before money, you'll still be battling with it after money. The only thing money changes are the ability to pay your bills, but if your soul is not in that abundant enlightenment state naturally, then internal struggle will continue.

The physical life is challenging to navigate when you're stuck in a physical vessel having to do physical chores day after day with no end in sight. It takes work and discipline to get to that space where you are truly comfortable with life inside and out. This is where you have been blessed enough to be able to create the life you've always dreamed of. Having those dreams is a great start, so don't let anyone squelch them or tell you they're impossible.

I had people tell me I couldn't do certain things, but then I'd accomplish them and suddenly everyone was silent and speechless. When they were saying I couldn't do certain things, what they really meant was that they couldn't do them. Usually people are talking about themselves when they say you can't accomplish something. They may look at achieving in a limited way, but that doesn't mean you need to fall for that fiction. Everything and anything is possible as long as you work hard to achieve it. It's not going to suddenly come crashing through the ceiling. It takes resilience and hard work to achieve a life you desire.

You can buy self-help spiritual books like this one, oracle and tarot decks, go to a psychic or angel reader, purchase crystals, candles, and incense. This doesn't mean that will manifest great things. All of those things can certainly help in some positive way by offering empowering tools, motivation, and information that can inspire you to feel good about where you are at and what's to come. It is up to you to take those action steps and work hard to reach for what you want. Don't let your life pass you by without putting in an effort fighting for your life and going after what you want. Many are aiming and struggling to achieve blissful happiness, which includes building their own personal blissful utopia. Never feel guilty for desiring, aiming, and fighting to be happy.

Why would someone want to live a life of misery? There are a great number of people threaded throughout the planet that enjoys living in misery and maintaining a negative disposition. Take a look at some of your colleagues, friends, or people you know to determine which ones whose life force is gone. Now they're a miserable vessel moving about accepting that this is their life. It's not what they might have imagined, but they've reached that point of having given up on life.

Social media is an exceptional place to visit if you need proof of the overall general disposition of people today. In fact, more people than not are hooked on living joyless lives. You might think otherwise, but this is permanently evident if you log onto a social media account and see the diatribe of negativity posted up about how someone hates a politician or a celebrity. This trait is unmistakable whenever you read a news story. Many news pieces are bathed in pessimism or destructive blather intended to entice and rattle the ego rather than inform and educate. News stories come off like unbalanced gossip pieces rather than an objective, neutral, balanced, and emotionally detached reporting of facts.

For those seeking to positively improve their lives and raise their consciousness, they do their best to frequently study up and educate themselves on any genre possible, including the areas they would never dive into. When you want to improve your life, you listen to or read stories from those that achieved success and how they did it. You read inspirational spiritually based books in hopes of getting inspired and motivated as a reminder that you can do it too. This is because you are just as worthy and capable of achieving your desires as any other soul being.

CHAPTER FOUR

Soul Growth, Visualization Foresight, Getting Optimistic and Taking Action

*E*very time you learn lessons that propel your soul forward spiritual growth is achieved. It is the knowledge gained through each experience that contributes to progress. This is regardless if the experience is challenging or positively enjoyable. It will still add to molding, shaping, and expanding your consciousness to greater heights. Sitting around in front of the television all day everyday accomplishing nothing of value will ensure your soul's growth remains in the same place. The exception to that is if someone is an invalid or battling a health issue. The health issue in this case is offering mental struggles and will power that strengthen and grow your soul. The opposite kind is if you plop on the sofa staring at trash television all day out of laziness.

You cannot watch reality television regularly or read gossip content on a daily basis and raise your conscious. This doesn't mean you have to avoid those things if you have interest in them. Because it's considered an unhealthy addiction due to the dumbed down content that enforces a stereotypical shallow existence, it is also having that same effect on your soul. This is about the offenders that spend their days absorbing this energy with no interest in anything else.

Raising your consciousness is important because remaining stunted in terms of soul growth ensures that karma is built up and an Earthly life do over in a tougher circumstance is inevitable. God sees that the one life run was wasted and didn't work. Having to do it again in a tougher circumstance life situation has a greater chance of placing enough Earthly life challenges to help your soul be snapped into long term soul reality that there is something greater at play than the Earthly life mundane that human beings set up. This is the same as a Wise One task master Teacher in school that gives the students a harder test than the one before in order to challenge them. This isn't done in punishment, but to help them grow and expand their mind and consciousness so they may graduate into something grander than where they are now.

There isn't one main event that assists in your spiritual growth, but numerous mini-events interwoven into your Earthly life. Major events will offer larger growth experiences, but the mini-events are just as important if not more so. The side effect to the events is that it helps you make sounder decisions, which help you live a more prosperous and abundant life.

GETTING OPTIMISTIC

One of the tasks to put into practice towards bringing in abundance is working on altering your perception into a positive mindset. This simple easy reminder is needed for when you stray too far off into negativity that it becomes your newly adopted personality trait. Positivity equates to you being a stronger abundance attractor, while reinforcing your connection with your Spirit team. This is because positivity and optimism reside in the higher vibrational energy field. It is the high vibrational state that allows an effortless connection with God.

Raising your consciousness simultaneously raises your vibration giving you a deeper awareness. This impeccable mindfulness helps in identifying the subtle cues coming in from the Divine that go unnoticed within and around you. Those cues are important because that communication is what is guiding you towards your purposes that need to be fulfilled in your lifetime. It is what prompts you to take notice of when a shift in thinking and feeling processes on your part is necessary. You were born able to access Divine communication effortlessly, but over time blocks rose up in your life that prevented you from having a crystal clear connection with God and your Spirit team. One of the tasks of a spirit guide is to guide you through life to help it be less friction oriented, than it would be if they weren't around. They guide you towards experiences they know will help shape, mold, and evolve your soul. They want to see the student snap into soul reality and suddenly become blissfully aware of all that is greater than the limited of the superficial. This requires your work to tune into them and heed their guidance.

Having spent my lifetime studying the human condition to the point of hair splitting, I've noticed that those who are believers in a higher power and remain in that state have less of a hard time in life than those that don't believe. This doesn't mean that those who are believers are problem free, but life is not as dramatic without that connection. It's also why gossips and those that love drama seem to have little to no spirit connection while in that state. Their life also seems to be filled with daily negativity and drama.

VISUALIZATION FORESIGHT

Another way to achieve abundance is to put it in your mind that you will obtain what you desire.

This is pending that what you desire is not harmful to your well-being or another person's. It will be something that is beneficial for your higher self's goal and soul's growth. Nothing should stop you from achieving and positively attracting good stuff pending it's not harming yourself or another.

Fears, insecurities, or low self-esteem are abundance success killers. They were born out of the darkness of ego and the human development stage. God and higher evolved beings don't entertain the lower energy, even though there are religious groups that focus on those lower energy elements and then say it's from God. I don't know any God that enjoys the evil and darkness of lower energy. The lower energy is of the Devil and has the intent of sabotaging and criminalizing you. Occasional fears will creep in on you on occasion, but when that's all that plagues your mind daily dominating your thoughts, then it will take over and do its best to destroy your goal. The goal of the Darkness is to stop you from finding the Light. It will do this in ways that convince you that you're unworthy. Avoid allowing negativity to take over and drown you.

Another way to attract in good stuff is by believing you already have what you want. Even when it seems impossible to enter your life, imagine it's a part of your life now. In your mind, close your eyes, and visualize it in motion. Feel it in every crevice of your cells as if it's happening now. Feel the good feelings associated with how you would feel having what you desire. This energy expands and spills into your reality by helping to make it happen from this visualization. This visualization is something that should be done regularly until you have what you desire.

If you desire to buy your own house one day, then begin the visualization of having this house. You can close your eyes at least once a day and envision what this house will look like. You'll visualize its surroundings, the kinds of neighbors that are around you, the location, and everything about it. You'll then visualize yourself living in this house, walking around throughout it, sleeping in your bed in this house, making a meal in the kitchen, the kinds of friends you have visiting this house, or the love partner that is with you in this house, and so on. Notice your feelings and state of mind and how you'll feel while living in this house as this is happening.

You can apply this visualization exercise to whatever you desire, whether it's a love relationship, job, car, or anything you desire. This is pending it is aligned with your higher self's purpose and God's will. The benefits to this visualization exercise are that it programs your mind to move away from the doubts and fears that you'll attract this in. It also assists in getting the positive energy surrounding this visualization towards making it happen.

When you wallow in negative feelings and thoughts that you'll never attract in what you desire, then this creates a separation between yourself and this desire that grows wider and further away from you. When you think good stuff associated with this desire, then it starts to bring the aspiration closer to you through this energy. You're already creating with your thoughts and feelings anyway, so you may as well make it positive oriented.

GET HAPPY NOW
AND THE REST WILL FOLLOW

Getting positive and optimistic isn't about covering up your negative thoughts with phony positive ones. The positive thoughts and feelings need to be authentic and unforced, otherwise it's just a negativity mask in disguise like hiding a cut behind a Band-Aid. Feel the good energy by partaking in fun healthy activities that you know will raise your vibration. Feeling positive thoughts and feelings authentically is experiencing those vibrations inside you.

Ask for Heavenly intervention and help through prayer, then pay attention to the guidance you're expected to take action on and take that action. You may not receive an answer at the time you're praying, but ask God and your Spirit team to show you signs of what to do. Request that they continuously reveal this answer in a way that you can recognize it.

Divine guidance will usually come to you three times or more. It repeatedly enters your auric field through your clair senses in hopes you'll discover that it's a message. This is all part of why it's important to adopt many of the guidance messages I've provided here and in some of my other spiritual books. It's not said to ruin your life, bring you down, or spoil your fun. This is all said because we know this is what will contribute to you having a stronger psychic clair sense channel with God and your Spirit team. When your psychic senses are strong, then you're more likely to pick up on the messages coming in. Your Spirit team will continue to give you the same signs until you notice it. You have free will choice to try it out or disregard it.

I had to learn all of this hard the way, because I was once an addicted party boy in my early twenties doing anything and everything toxic I could get my hands onto.

Bring in what you desire by allowing it to flow towards you naturally. You're not chasing your dreams in a panic. You're taking productive action steps through methodical movements with love to obtain what you long for. If there's someone you're interested in romantically, then ask them out whether or not you're male or female. Regardless of their answer, don't chase or burden them by staying on top of them relentlessly. When it's the right one, it will flow and merge with you naturally and organically. Placing any kind of demands will push it away. The same goes for work related endeavors or anything you have your eyes set on. The serious relationships I've had over the course of my life all transpired without effort. It came to be when I wasn't looking or longing, but when I was content. When I was frustrated or in a negative mindset, nothing came to pass.

Actress Nicole Kidman once said there was a time when her fantasy life was richer than her reality. She dove into working on back-to-back films because her real life outside of work was less than she originally hoped. Over time, this was reversed where her real life became everything she dreamed of with the house, husband, and family. Those particular things may not be of interest to you, but the point was that she escaped into work not realizing these other things outside of that were being moved into position. She worked hard and the rewards she desired eventually one day came.

If you continuously fall into a negative mindset, then be aware of when that happens and mentally tell yourself something like, *"I need to adjust the vibration levels of my thinking."*

Follow that with shifting and raising the negative direction of your thoughts into optimistic ones. When you've been wallowing in negativity, then that can block good stuff from flowing to you. It's easy to fall into despair and frustration when enormous time has passed, and your desires haven't manifested into reality. When you look back on the passing time, it seems that nothing in your life has changed. You feel stagnant like being indefinitely stuck in the mud. You crave positive change and stimulation, but good stuff ceases to flow in. There isn't anything bad or negative happening in your life, which is a blessing that isn't often appreciated, but there is zero movement with anything at all. You are not where you thought or envisioned you would be five years prior. This can put a damper on your faith as you wonder what you've been doing wrong. When this happens, revert back to faith and prayer to help re-align your soul.

FOLLOW DIVINE GUIDANCE THROUGH ACTION

You may start to fear that Spirit and Heaven are ignoring you or perhaps the non-movement is out of your hands. Consider the possibility that Spirit is diligently working behind the scenes throughout that entire time and have not had much luck getting things moving for you. They have to work with other people's free will choices that go against what is intended to take place. They're also putting up signs, guidance, and messages for you or others to take action on. You or another might be ignoring those action steps, sometimes for years thus no movement happens during that time. They can't reveal the next step until the first action step they've been throwing in front of you is taken. It doesn't matter if that action step takes one month or ten years. The same repetitive action step will keep popping up in front of you for a reason until you notice it and take action on it.

There can be cases where you have been putting in the tireless work and action steps. There is nothing you did wrong to cause your life to feel forever stationary. There could be other factors at play to consider. Some of that might be the maneuvering of the puzzle pieces your Spirit team is attempting to orchestrate to help move things along. There are also the free will choices you or another party is choosing that go against what Spirit is recommending. This is another reason that many of the teachings in my work are discussed. It's because they all play a part at helping those interested in becoming clearer vessels for God. It's ultimately for your soul's benefit.

It took me seven years to get into the film business. I was sixteen years old when I knew that was going to be my next big move. It wasn't until I turned twenty-three years old when it worked out in my favor. That's seven years of what felt like stagnancy. What did I do during that time? I obtained my first regular job as a teenager at the record store chain when those existed. I simultaneously studied up on the creative side of the film business, I read and wrote in journals, I experienced life, perfected my resume, made lists of entertainment production companies and contacted them. My general disposition was that I was going to get in and nothing was going to stop me. I said, "I will never stop trying to get in. I will keep doing that until I'm eighty, I don't care."

I had the occasional doubt or frustration with, "This is ridiculous. When is it going to happen?"

Those negative moments were rare, because that wasn't my general disposition. 95% of the time I was focused on getting in with excitement. I kept working hard to achieve it, then by some sheer force of miracle from above I got in. What are the odds that a movie star is going to hire some young punk kid with no experience? Unlikely. There was regular praying and taking action steps on my part until one day I received that surprise call back.

In fact, when the call came in I was so stunned that it took me an hour to center myself before calling back. It seemed too good to be true that I went into this hazy state of shock not believing it. The point of sharing that tidbit of a story was that I was no one in particular, without any experience, but myself to sell. This means that anybody has the capability of doing it if they have passion, persistence, hard work, and a great attitude.

After talking to me, the production company discovered that underneath that punk rebellious aura there was a super high intellect that dominated the bosses. This was considered a strength and asset to the company. Use who you are, your personality, and those parts of you to showcase to the world. People love authenticity and originality. Those that make big decisions such as hiring gravitate towards someone who is different than the norm.

What you can do before you do anything is change your thoughts and get positive. Look at the bright side of what you have in your life today. Take a second and allow the good stuff to flush through you now. Visualize what you desire to see in your life, get optimistic and excited about it, ask for help from above, and then take action and work hard to achieve it.

Chapter Five

Give Yourself a Break

Remove anything and everything that is a mindless distraction from your higher priorities. If you have work to do, action steps you need to take to improve your life, make something important happen, then get to work. Notice how much time is spent during your day with mindless activities. For many people, the immediate and obvious answer is social media or internet surfing.

Social media can become addicting where you find you're posting nonsense, or scrolling and surfing all day long when you know you have work to do. It's one thing to take a mindless break for an hour, but another to spend hours online achieving nothing. It's the ego's way of coaxing you into wasting time.

Other time wasters can include chatting on dating/sex apps with people you rarely meet or have no interest in building a long lasting connection with. This doesn't mean chatting with potentials has any harm. You can't get closer to meeting the one for you if you're not out there mingling. There is a fine line between being proactive in getting to know quality people on an app over chatting with numerous people out of boredom or loneliness.

Time wasters can also fall into addictions such as food, drugs, sex, and/or alcohol. This isn't the same as getting together with friends on a Saturday night for a drink. This is about the daily time-wasting activities you devote towards each day, instead of contributing productively with action steps towards your dreams.

I've been guilty of all that too in the past. I've complained that nothing is improving or changing in my life, but then I take a step back to evaluate what I've been doing each day, and it's a bunch of mindless time wasters. Time wasters are a great distraction when you've been putting in too much productivity that it's caused burn out or exhaustion. A much needed break away into something mindless and relaxing is needed. This is about doing too much of one over the other, which creates imbalance. Imbalance is another abundance killer.

Incorporate nature outings into your life at least once a week, if not once a day. Many lead incredibly busy work lives where they're lucky if they hit a nature setting once a month. Others may not even consider going into a nature locale or understand why they should. I remember seeing some comedy film where the character was from a busy chaotic city and ended up in nature where she complained that she couldn't breathe, as the air was too clean and fresh. It was done for humor, but there are people who do feel that way or unaware of the health well-being benefits of nature. They might find it boring because there isn't a bar there.

Some may have the luxury of living in a home with a backyard filled with nature, while others need to venture off to a nature locale. The ones that need to get in the car or on foot to travel to the nature patch will put it off. Weeks have gone by and they have yet to take a walk or exercise in nature, let alone at least around the block. This can be due to procrastination, laziness, and sometimes due to having agoraphobia, which I also personally understand. This is that unnatural fear that prevents you from venturing outside, as you're afraid it may induce some kind of panic.

As someone plagued with social anxiety, there are exercises I have to do before I head outside. I push myself to do it daily no matter what. Take deep breaths in, center yourself, and call in Archangel Michael to extricate the fear and get you out there. Ask a friend to go with you if that helps motivate you to venture to a nature patch to feel the Divine energy.

Nature is filled with high vibrational spirit beings than any other location on the planet. When you stroll through a park on your mental health walk or jog you can feel the stresses lifting off your body. A wave of focused energy and clarity opens up where brilliant ideas, feelings, and thoughts reveal themselves to you. Nature is a therapeutic setting where the angels and high vibrational spirits are able to effortlessly work on you by helping to raise your vibration. They lower their vibration to meet yours and the psychic connection is made.

When I bike down to my beach regularly, I notice the shift as soon as I reach the top of the hill where I can see the ocean. A strong sea breeze slams into me and I'm suddenly soaring above the universe. People in big cities live on top of each other, which is not conducive or beneficial on your health and well-being. You have to work extra hard to find a nature setting with little to no people where you can clear your mind.

New York City is considered the highest populated city in America, which is hard to believe considering it's a small area. They might have a harder time, because even the parks are crowded. Los Angeles has the beaches if you're able to find a little patch of space all to yourself with no people. You'll be lucky to find such a place outside of the Summer months. It's better to hit those nature settings than not to, regardless if it's packed with people or not.

Crystal clear clarity rises in its visibility when you're in nature. Many people sit in cold corporate like boxes all day each week, only to go home in a cold travelling box. All of this crushes your soul's life force. It's not a place for creative thinking, which is required by all souls including business professionals.

Does your life, job, or career role have you sitting all day? You may notice that around 2-2:30-ish in the afternoon when you suddenly feel a surge of fatigue and exhaustion and can't figure out why. When there is no other underlying medical issue, then it can be that your body is releasing melatonin telling you it's time to take a catnap. Unfortunately, many work at jobs where that is impossible, so instead you force yourself awake with caffeine to keep going. It's like the "Clockwork Orange" film where you're forcing your eyes open. I've had people tell me they sleep in their cars on their break. They will find ways to squeeze that mid-day rest in.

Avoid eating lunch at your desk if you work in an office, unless you plan to get outside afterwards for fresh air and a stroll. Sitting at your desk all day long indefinitely for months and years is horrible on your health, well-being, creativity, and productivity. In past jobs, I remember witnessing employees who basically sat at their desk from the time they arrived until they clocked out. I'd approach them to ask if they've been outside. They would inform me they haven't. I'd suggest going out for a walk for air and come back refreshed. I'll even go with them for company if they want. This would excitedly get them going.

Some believe you should continue to work all through lunch. They think it's cool to push people into slavery. I've been working my entire life and considered a hard worker by all I come across, but that's because I incorporate regular breaks. I don't believe in working until you drop. It's working smarter. You don't work yourself or employees into the ground. You take an actual lunch and head outside, get some fresh air, walk around, come back to work re-energized. That is what will boost your energy, productivity, and creativity levels, while lowering stress at the same time. Taking frequent breaks are the law in many areas, so that people don't experience this burnout and don't fall into a slave mentality.

When you wake up at say 730am and proceed to get ready to start your day, then you may not be in bed until around 11 pm that night if you're lucky. That's a super long time to be awake, functioning, and turned "on" through the day. It's no surprise everyone faces daily exhaustion from students to busy career professionals. You keep pumping yourself up with caffeine to keep going because this current life set up by naïve human beings doesn't allow a true honest midday break to rest and exercise before diving back into work.

There was a time that caffeine fixes didn't exist. People woke up as the sun rose, they worked outdoors in the clean air of nature, they took those frequent breaks, their diets were better, stress was less invasive, and they went to bed when the sun went down. Human beings invented some great things such as caffeine, but too much of a good thing as you know can backfire causing you the opposite effect of what you hoped it would do.

When you need a toxic addiction to cope and get through it, it's best to keep it on lower levels and in moderation. As per usual, I learned that the hard way, so I understand what it's like to have that kind of addiction.

In the past, when people set and designed things, they never considered the human souls well-being and overall capabilities and limitations. People used to praise someone for being able to work for fifteen hours a day without stopping. There's nothing admirable about that anymore. Now someone feels bad for those who don't know how to stop and relax. Many of the rules that exist today were created eons ago during a time when they worked. They haven't been changed since to accommodate how life has become today. This is why so many people are unhappy and complaining throughout each day.

To raise your vibration and become a strong abundance attractor, you must be disciplined about what you consume and how you set up your surroundings. Focusing on clean healthy diets as much as possible is beneficial to your health and spiritual connection with Heaven. All of this is what positively gives you more energy to work on the projects and endeavors that matter. You can let loose and have fun occasionally going for that Pizza and Beer night, but this is about your overall diet and toxic intake and how that affects your day.

It's challenging for many to change their diets to something cleaner, unprocessed, or chemical free, especially if you're a 9-6 Monday thru Friday corporate professional. While it is possible to improve your diet, it can still be challenging for a great number of people. When you are consuming cleaner foods, then your body, mind, and soul notice the difference gradually over time. There are many advocates for cleaner foods and diets, but they may not have begun making those changes until after they were successful. You can incorporate small important changes with all of this gradually, rather than making these massive changes all at once in the same day. You adopt new positive regimens to your life slowly by bringing in the change little by little, so that it doesn't feel challenging and overwhelming. This is the same process if you want to quit a toxin. You don't worry about quitting cold turkey and not being able to sustain it. You work on using the toxin less and less over time.

For example, if someone wanted to quit drinking wine daily, then you cut the wine drinking to half a glass rather than a full glass. You work on skipping a day by not touching any wine, even if you have one the next day. You gradually spread it out to the point it's not everyday, but every other day, then every couple days, to every week, to every month, until you're no longer craving it. If you relapse after months of not having the toxin and end up reaching for the toxin, then don't beat yourself up about it, but let it go and start again the next day.

I've noticed and experienced positive changes within and around me when I did my best to consume cleaner foods and drinks. This doesn't mean I don't have fun once in awhile with that bad food or drink, but I'm conscious of what I'm consuming overall. The saying is true that you are what you eat. If you're eating bad foods all day long, then you cut off the psychic spiritual connection with the other side. If you don't want to hear God, then eat a whole pizza and some ice cream. You won't pick up on anything from the other side for the rest of the day.

CHAPTER SIX

Detox, Clearing, Motivation

*M*any sensitive's shy away or keep away from other people due to the negativity that they often associate with other people. It may not be that every person is bathed in negative energy, but a highly sensitive person is more prone to absorbing every shred of energy from all that it crosses path with that it can become unbearable. Some might call them anti-social or shy, which is the not thought out point of view and goes much deeper. Not everyone is bouncing off the walls in extroverted spirits. Every person on the planet has a built in composite of personality traits that they're born with, such as astrological, or it's molded into them by the events during their childhood. The highly sensitive person ends up seeing all people as risky to be near, even though there are good and bad energies within every person that exists. Because they sense every nuance, they absorb these energies that people emanate off of them more than other souls do.

There are good people threaded in the mix of the negative, but because both energies are so potent, the highly sensitive person is overwhelmed by the massive energies that dart towards them that it leaves them temporarily drained. Going to crowded places like a mall, amusement park, or grocery store can wear them out. This is why they have to run their life like a strict disciplined executive ensuring their soul and sensitive nature are protected. They learn to be careful about the decisions they make each day that could have an effect on their well-being. This is one of the pluses of being a highly sensitive person. It's that you're more likely to have a keen clairsentient clear feeling psychic channel that you can detect what to stay away from. While another person that isn't as in tune will dive right into danger oblivious of the consequences.

Detoxing your world when it comes to people means being mindful of who you allow into your auric circle. Keep those you see as antagonistic away from you or in small doses if you have no choice. Those you have no choice but to see might be family members or work colleagues. Surround yourself with optimistic positive people whenever possible.

When two positive optimistic go-getters join forces, then there is no telling how far you can both go. You feel inspired by one another, rather than brought down by them. Some of the personality types that can contribute to lowering your vibration just by being in their vicinity can be a gossip, negative complainer, or someone who regularly makes toxic choices. When you're around someone like that everyday, then this can unknowingly have an effect on you being a positive abundance attractor.

You may be a naturally positive person and feel you're doing everything possible to attract in good stuff, but find that nothing good comes in. One of the blocks preventing this good stuff from coming in can be something you were unaware of such as being around negative people. This will have an effect on what you are attracting into your life.

Being around a Debby Downer will only bring you down. It will also stall you from moving forward. Focus on quality people to surround yourself with such as those who are mutually supportive of you as you are with them. They also allow you the required space you need throughout each day because they understand that you are a sensitive. Highly sensitive people need more time outs alone than others.

Eliminating toxic friendships also includes those on your social media page. The world is drama ridden and chaotic enough with all the daily gossip noise from politically hyped chatter to celebrity gossip. You've likely noticed whenever the latest scandal rises that every other person will post non-constructive words that come out in a negative toxic scream, whine, or complaint about the target. This does nothing to help anyone. It's toxic energy that fans those flames undeserving of attention. It brings you down, it lowers your vibration, it blocks good stuff from coming to you, and it puts a damper on your life. You then carry that out in the world and spread that to whomever you connect with. Those you pass it to then take that energy and spread it around as well. Soon the entire planet has erupted into nonsensical chaos that helps no one at all.

This isn't just practical advice from Spirit, but those sensitive and more in-tune than others have all vocally expressed having noticed this on their own. They know how it ultimately makes them feel, which isn't a positive uplifting feeling.

I've watched past acquaintances and friends on social media announce that their wall thread is too plagued with negative energy that they plan to take a break from social media. That's one of the great ways to detox from technology for a bit, but at the same time you shouldn't have to run and hide from your own page. Instead you can hide that toxic persons posts or remove them altogether. Some have gone as far as to deleting their account, which might seem extreme. There are ways around that if you want to stay on social media. This is by being exceptionally careful about the types of people you're allowing on your friend list.

One of the positive new tools available on some

social media sites now is you can unfriend people if you choose, or unfollow them if you don't want to unfriend them. This way you can keep them in your friends list, but you no longer see their posts. This is beneficial for someone you like, but you can't stand the constant negative posts they keep putting up. I did this myself with people that continuously posted negative posts on the politicians and celebrities they hate everyday all day long.

Popular social media sites at this point are Facebook, Instagram, and Twitter. All three now have this 'hide' feature. Many social media sites are aware this is a problem, so the fact that my Spirit team and I are discussing it is nothing new. If at the time you're reading this, none of those social media sites are around, there is likely something similar available that can apply to this.

It's rare for someone to post about the positives they like about someone. It's easier for the ego to gossip about who they hate. When someone is unhappy or unaligned, then they are more apt to posting negativity. Happy centered people aren't attracted to negativity and prefer to post constructive positive content.

By the time I was done hiding the repeat offenders on social media, I had a nice clean uplifting page with people who posted more engaging interesting content that was on the positive side. Letting go of negativity allows room for positivity. Positivity brings more positivity.

When detoxing from people and social media, you also want to detox from distractions and time wasters. These are distractions that eat up good chunks of your day from wasteful internet and social media surfing to chatting with random people on dating apps that you don't care all that much about. This is knowing that you have work to do or that you could be doing. It's not a crime to have a guilty pleasure you enjoy breaking away to for some fun, such as random internet surfing to chatting with others on a dating app. Chatting out of boredom daily, rather than chatting with someone you genuinely have an interest in knowing, can lead to more procrastination.

CLEAR THE CLUTTER

Clearing the clutter is part of organizing. It's included as part of the detoxing process. Detoxing all aspects of your life prepares you to open the gates to abundance. The clutter clearing is beneficial since it cleans the energy and allows you to focus more clearly. Clear focus equates to a stronger communication connection with your Spirit team. As a writer, I will incorporate procrastination techniques where I need to make sure my space is completely clear of clutter before I fall into the zone to write.

When you walk into a messy room you immediately sense the chaos, which makes your thinking more chaotic and unsettled. Clear away the cobwebs and the clutter by boxing up or throwing away items you will never need or look at again. If it has deep sentimental value or attachment and you're not ready to part with it, then box it up and put it in a closet or storage if it doesn't need to be lying around.

Commit to simplicity and keep your surroundings organized and uncluttered. Extricate friendships that you don't consider to be true authentic friendships, but connections you keep around due to a fear of loneliness. If the friendship stresses you out, then it's time to begin distancing yourself from them. Friendships that are true and long lasting will place no demands on you or your time. They understand this and form naturally unfettered.

This all has an effect on the energy you're creating in your life. If your life has some unseen negative dents in it, then this can create a block to attracting in good stuff.

Detoxing your inner and outer worlds isn't just about detoxing your body of toxic addictions, bad foods, drugs, or alcohol. It's more than going on a fast or cleanse. It's also about detoxing every aspect of your life from clearing the clutter in your home and work life to detoxing the people around you. Do a thorough examination of the people in your world from family to friendships. Who brings you down whenever they come around? Work on eliminating and dissolving those in your life that do nothing, but bring drama and chaos to your world. Even if you don't extricate them, eventually the angels will remove people from your life that have fulfilled their purpose or contribute nothing of positive benefit, but stall you from moving forward. You don't have to wipe out best friendships or family members that you love on some level, but you keep contact with them in small doses. Generally, when someone isn't a fan of a family member, they're usually not spending every mind numbing minute with them.

Get structured in your life and plan, schedule, and organize your surroundings. When you have a clear space, you have a clear mind. A clear mind helps you get focused while allowing your Spirit team's wisdom, messages, and guidance to come flowing in. This guidance helps bring you one step closer to achieving what you desire.

Be mindful of the daily or weekly purchases you make. There is a fine line between overspending on things you don't need, to buying the occasional gadget or item you would love to have. Buying something for you is part of self-care. It's when it moves into constant frivolous financial spending to fill an emotional void that you begin to block the flow of abundance. You may already know when you're spend-happy to make you feel better. When it becomes a regular habit, then it moves into toxic territory that can have an effect on what you're bringing into your life. Every atom, cell, and matter that exists is energy, regardless if it's physical material items or part of your feelings and thoughts. Breathe new life into all of the energy cells in your world to becoming a clear vessel of reception with God. All wonderful things end up coming out of that.

GET MOTIVATED TO SUCCEED

You might have other distractions such as work or family obligations that seem to eat up your time each day. This is to the point that you have zero time to devote towards your life purpose, passions, or in building your side business. That side business is the one that will eventually free you from the confinement restrictions of being unemployed or from working day jobs you despise. Daily procrastination techniques and distractions can eventually make you notice that a week has gone by where you've donated zero time towards your purpose. Sometimes your ego will have you push that away when realistically you could squeeze in a half hour to an hour each day that consists of one action step towards your passion and purpose.

In the past, I've made excuses that there isn't any time. After weeks of that I started to pay more attention to the downtime I did have. I'd say, "I have forty-five minutes with nothing to do before I need to leave for my dinner. I can squeeze in something important now."

All souls on the planet are worthy and deserving of blessings as any other. When you get into a position where you feel blessed for the good you have now, then this lifts your energy vibration to welcome in more. It also allows you to do good stuff for others when you are no longer filled with other practical day-to-day worries. Once you're taken care of, then it's easier to freely focus on others who could use your helping hand.

Everyone is born with special gifts in the areas of psychic abilities to creative skills. There isn't one person on the planet that doesn't have something extraordinary about them to utilize and contribute towards the betterment of humanity. At the same time, many distinctly amazing people struggle in low vibrational jobs to physically survive that they end up pushing their authentic talents down to continue on. The angels want to guide them out of that and can help maneuver circumstances to produce blessings to propel that soul forward. It can take them years to decades to help some people, while it seems others are blessed at an early age. It doesn't mean you're less talented or gifted than someone else.

Each person is a special case with varying reasons as to what the delays or blocks are. This is another reason clearing and detoxing your world is beneficial. It helps you become a stronger conduit with the Divine. When that takes place, then you're able to detect the answers clearly as to what is preventing the positive flow of abundance enlightenment.

Avoid placing a time limit on when good things can or will happen. It doesn't matter how old you are, as you are not discriminated against from receiving blessings and miracles at any age. There are numerous factors that have to be considered that come into play as to why there are delays to witnessing a positive flow of abundance. Some of those factors require work on your part.

An older person might feel resentment when they see a twenty-two year old popular well-known entertainer purchase a mansion worth three million along the coast with a magnificent view. This doesn't mean this popular star is any more deserving or worthy of excessive material abundance over you. In one sense, it might feel like the luck of the draw, or that the maneuvering your Spirit team has been working on behind the scenes is taking longer than another person. It's super easy to fall into envy and resentment in that instance, especially if you've been working so hard and yet are seeing little to no return in the hard working investment you've been applying for years. Believe me I understand, and so does Spirit, but you don't want to wallow too deeply in that energy indefinitely as that will block what needs to come in.

The other side of that is you don't know the challenges and tough experiences the popular star is faced with behind closed doors. You may say you don't care, but despite their fat bank account, they could be battling with issues far worse than you could imagine. Some find it difficult to sympathize with anyone who doesn't have money issues, but when you do that then you're placing higher value on money. That person with money is human like anyone else and going through personal challenges you're unaware of. What matters to Heaven is what is in your heart and who you are regardless of what's in your bank account.

Heaven is also dealing with people that operate primarily from ego and free will. Your Spirit team could be frequently attempting to get the attention of someone important on Earth that can propel you forward, but that person is not picking up on the guidance. You suffer longer because the person intended to make an important offer to you that can change your life is not following the hunches periodically put in front of them. It can also be you who isn't noticing the guidance coming in or following. All of that can create an immense amount of delays.

Due to human free will choices consistently getting in the way of conclusive progress can create an enormous amount of delays to seeing your hard work not reap much reward. Never give up, never lose faith, and never stop believing. Keep telling yourself the breakthrough will come and it will on the wings of Angels. And so it is.

CHAPTER SEVEN

*Smart Money Management: Pay Off Debts,
Save for Retirement, Donate and Give*

*P*aying off debts is also included in the detox clearing the clutter process. It is essential to balancing the energy in your life. With balanced energy derives abundance, blessings, and miracles. Struggling to get out of debt can create a damper on your life. It can lower your vibration when the stress is so great that it starts to mess with your emotions. Paying off your debts for certain things can be done even if it's a small amount each month.

In the film *Parenthood*, the Jason Robards character says a truthful statement to his son who owed money to some bad people. He said, "If they are business people, they'll be happy to get something rather than nothing."

This method of paying just a tiny bit will also gradually move you one tiny step towards getting out of debt, even if it's just five dollars. Don't use more of your credit than you don't have. If you have a credit card and the credit card company offers to raise your limit, then don't sign up for that. It will only trap you by increasing your interest and payments per month. You'll be tempted to buy more than you have. Naturally, this would seem like common sense, but you understand that so many people with credit don't follow that rule.

It's easy to go crazy with spending when you are under the impression you have the money. Just because your credit card company may say you have that spending limit, it doesn't mean you have that money. Spend what you know you can easily pay back sooner than later. Don't feel overwhelmed by gazing at the large number you owe, but instead cut back on spending and increase your payments, even if it's a small amount each pay period.

If you're trying to build credit or increase your credit score, then save the credit card for smaller purchases such as gas for your car. Pay back more than you've spent. Paying off your credit card in one gigantic lump sum can surprisingly drop your score, so keep an eye on that.

Getting out of debt can also be an emotional

debt as well where you're obliged to another person that brings you negativity and grief. They offer nothing in the way of positivity. You're left wondering how to extricate them from your life. This can be done through a gradual dissolving where you're less available for them over time. It's your life and you are the owner of this life. Don't allow anyone to dominate or over power you by making you do things you're not interested in doing.

SAVING FOR RETIREMENT

One of the top concerns human beings have while experiencing an Earthly life is security. People work to make money to be able to physically survive and be secure. This includes the security of a positive home life, the security of a relationship, the security of friendships, the security of family. Security is a big deal to human beings because this is a practical world that requires security to thrive. Don't forget the most important security comes from the abundance enlightenment you receive through your faith in a higher power.

Most everyone wants to feel safe and comfortable to one degree or another. Some people work to be able to pay for rent, food, clothing, as well as other practical necessities, while others add an additional concern onto that which is having their eye further out into the future. They want to make sure they'll be okay when they reach retirement age. This is something that not all think about until it's too late. When you're twenty-three, it's less than likely that you'll be thinking much about retirement as opposed to being forty-three.

When should you be thinking about where you'll be when you reach retirement age? The answer is right away.

At the end of the day, most people are working to have security, to pay their bills, and live comfortably without any fear of not having money. Yet, many people find they work paycheck to paycheck where most of it goes to their expenses. There isn't much left over to put aside for that rainy day.

Avoid waiting until the last minute to start saving money for retirement. Start as soon as possible even if it's just $5.00 a week, or whatever dollar conversion is used in the country you're reading this from. Five dollars a week does not sound like a ton of money, but if you start doing that at age 21, then by the time you're 41 you'll have an estimated $100,000. If you're 44, then you'll have that by age 84. If you put in more or you double that, then you'll have an estimated $200,000. This is all for putting away just $10 a week. You're also not including the other accounts you might have set up where you add a small amount to that too. This can be your 401K as well if you have one.

You don't think much of saving for retirement when you're moving through your twenties or maybe even your thirties, but as you grow older you'll wish you had. In my twenties, I had set up private savings accounts, retirement accounts, stock accounts, and other accounts from former jobs. Life moved on, the years continued forward, and I had forgot about looking into the accounts. When I did, I was astonished at how great the numbers were that accumulated in there. Basically, there was at least enough for a large down payment on a home if not more.

You can have those accounts set up in a way where it's automatically transferring money into the accounts, then you don't have to remember to do it every week, since it's likely you may forget. Time moves on and you go back to check one of the accounts as I did and you'll be thunderstruck to find that the amount increased.

I've had friends implement the methods I described. Months later they excitedly sent me screenshots from their accounts showing the amounts increasing. This gets them even more excited to see how easy it did that with such a low amount each week. It motivated them to start adding more.

When you think of having to save for the future you might think you don't have that kind of money to be putting hundreds of dollars or more into an account each week, let alone every month. When you understand that you could be putting away anything from $1.00-$5.00 minimum each week and that it would increase to a good chunk decades down the line, then you feel less overwhelmed about it. Some people waste $3-$5 a day on a fancy cup of coffee or tea. Go without that fancy cup at least once a week and put the money into a separate account instead.

You don't fear so much about where you'll be or what you'll have in terms of security when you reach a certain age. You could be employed for decades, but then there's that one day when you're laid off, fired, or the company closes up shop. You discover it's harder than ever trying to find a job in the new market when you're older.

Take into account there will be ever growing new adopted ways of working you hadn't been versed much in over the years because you didn't need to know about it. Perhaps an illness or disorder blocks you from working. Maybe you have trouble finding another job. Perhaps there is another issue that prevents income from coming in. You'll be glad and pleased with yourself to know that you had been saving a tiny amount on the side weekly that it becomes your saving grace years later. Don't fret no matter how old you are now. It's never too late to start implementing this strategy today. It doesn't matter if you're twenty or seventy. It's better to start late than to not do it at all.

One security measure to take into account is that you want to avoid putting all of your eggs in one basket. You might decide to only put money away into one investment account, but by some force of bad luck something should happen to that account, then you risk losing everything. While this is rare, it does and has happened in the past.

On a grand scale this happened with the Bernard Madoff story. Bernard Madoff was considered one of the top investors at his peak, until it was discovered that he was taking people's savings out of their accounts to shuffle it around. They called it one of the largest Ponzi schemes in history at the time. It's true many rich millionaires lost their money by him doing that, but there were also the working class folks who work paycheck to paycheck whose entire savings was in there. Some people ended up committing suicide. Finding out that after twenty years of working hard someone ran off with your money is devastating.

You can watch the Madoff story in, *The Wizard of Lies* with Robert DeNiro and Michelle Pfeiffer. Recommended films can convey a certain point that is helpful in one's life. Many therapists recommend films for homework towards healing as a matter of fact. Plus, most people tend to like movies, so it doesn't feel like work to sit through one if it's good. What happened with the Madoff story is rare, but this is one reason to ensure that you don't put all of your money in one place. Spread it out in different accounts even if it's just $5.00 a week in a couple of accounts. Contributing something in there is better than nothing.

As you organize your life, you increase the positive flow of energy, which equates to abundance flowing into your world. Organizing your life also includes organizing your finances. Many people live check to check, but you can still put away one to five dollars a week for life through savings or investments. You'd be surprised how low of an amount of that a week adds up to a great deal of change in ten to twenty years. Think about your future as soon as possible early on.

This isn't common to think about when you're

under thirty. It's as you move into your thirties and beyond do you later wish you invested earlier. Start as soon as possible even if it's just one dollar a week. There are many investment programs available through search engines that can help. Talk to your bank, a financial advisor, or investor. Check out Phone Apps like Acorn or Stash. Set up a Money Market account or a special Savings account with a bank. You can check on the equivalent in your own country or come up with your own methods of saving a little bit of money on the side each week.

If you have the personality where you know you'll start pulling money out of any of these accounts, then inquire with your bank about a locked account where they don't let you touch it for a set amount of years as it's accruing. This isn't hoarding, but saving for your future. Think about where you'll be in older age when finding a day job becomes harder to come by, or if you suddenly hit hard financial times later in life.

DONATING AND GIVING

Other ways of bringing more abundance to you is to look at what you are giving, donating, or putting out in the world. If what you put out into the world is negative or gossip filled, then that is the energy of what will boomerang right back to you. Donate to your favorite charity, even if all you can afford to spare is $1.00 a month. Giving something is better than nothing to keep the flow of abundance moving.

Donating with the motive of wanting something in return is not authentic giving. Donating to charities that have negative ulterior motives contributes negative energy as well, so you want to make sure the charity is positively beneficial. Most political campaigns to help someone with a candidacy can be negatively motivated and considered waste. Helping someone of lesser means on the economic scale to helping a child come out of abuse would fall into the positive contributions on that scale. Jesus Christ would help someone in need on the streets, before helping someone get elected into a political office.

Proposition 8 was a ballot initiative to ban same sex marriage in California in 2008. Those who supported or opposed it donated almost $100 million dollars. How much do you want to bet that those same people have never bothered to mobilize or donate that kind of money to help the poor, help children in need, prevent child abuse, or improve school curriculums to give people a better quality of life. It's far less than those that participated in preventing two people in love from marrying. Welcome to Earthly life created by human beings.

Donating something positive can be more than financial giving. It can be the donating of your time to help others in need. Finding ways to positively help others and offering the goodness of your heart goes along way. The angels see that as giving in the giving and receiving equation. When you sit around waiting to receive blessings and miracles, but offer nothing in return for that energy, then you'll be sitting around waiting for a long time. When you give or donate anything, it must be done without wanting in return.

There comes a point when good-hearted people that always give and get nothing in return will start to become resentful. As soon as you move into bitterness, then you have moved out of the positive energy flow of abundance. It's also a sign that you've created an imbalance by giving too much. Energy is a give and take exchange where there has to be an equal amount flowing back and forth.

You pay money to purchase goods, then that's a positive energy exchange. You're handing over something of worth for another thing of worth. This doesn't mean you halt giving permanently when nothing good has been forthcoming, but it does ask you to slow it down a bit to prevent you from moving into resentment territory. Pay attention to whom you are giving to and where it's needed. It's the same way you pick your battles as to what is a worthier noble cause or not. What calls for your warrior like energy to change something for the better or what requires you to ignore something and walk away.

Some people are interested in other causes and charities such as animal cruelty, environmental planet work, to finding cures for diseases and health issues. Giving positively of your time, energy, or money without the need or desire for something in return helps open the gates that will allow a healthy flow of abundance into your world.

Opening the floodgates of abundance requires much more from you than sitting around waiting for it to ring your doorbell. You need to be proactive and understand that making no decision or choice is making a choice. By choosing to be inactive, you have chosen.

There is enough room on the planet for every soul to be contributing positively towards the advancement of humanity where all can live in harmony. The world is hard enough to live on with all of the constant negativity and the darkness of ego running the show. You may feel as if you're alone in contributing your part, but you're not. There are millions of souls also doing their part. Rather than display jealousy, envy, or animosity towards those who bring positivity to the world, work on thinking up something positive to say about them. It's easier for the darkness of ego to criticize than to praise. Everyone that contributes positivity helps at least one person out there.

CHAPTER EIGHT

Does the Law of Attraction Work?

*T*he law of attraction was made popular in the spiritual communities, but the universal laws have been around on some level since the days of Christ. Some of the concepts of the law of attraction do and can work. This depends on someone's personal reality and where they are in their life. The laws are simple and easy enough to follow. If you don't put an effort into something, then nothing will happen. If you don't do your work at your job, then it won't get done.

One particular type of vitamin or medicine will not work the same way for every single person. It depends on that person's body chemistry. The laws of attraction work in that same way. Some of the concepts (medicine) within the laws of attraction work effortlessly for someone, but may not necessarily for another. The one it doesn't work for will write the whole law and the people that follow it as being insane and gullible, regardless that the laws are actually centuries old and have worked for millions of people over the course of that time.

Perhaps there are some that are gullible believing that something is working or happening when it isn't. What difference does it make if it brings the person out of misery and despondence and into joy and peace.

Someone takes an aspirin and an hour later says, "I'm feeling much better."

Another person takes an aspirin and hours later says, "I still feel miserable. This didn't work. Why did it work for you?"

The law of attraction and the spiritual and new age movement has drawn in millions of people who love it and feel comfortable with it, while millions of other people call it deceitful or erroneous. It may be nonsense to one person, but it isn't to someone else. There are the negative pessimists that go through life thinking, "If something is too good to be true, then it usually isn't true."

That may be the case for them, but doesn't mean that will be the case for you. Their life has never improved on any level regardless of what they've done, while many others have noticed positive changes within and around them for applying positive stuff into their life. Prefer to work on being positive than negative, since feeling good naturally and feeling positive and optimistic about something feels far much better than living in the abyss of negativity, pessimism, doubt and fear.

There are cases where someone will dramatically change their values over the course of their life. They might switch religions or political beliefs at some point, but it's typically not over night. It transpires and moves in that new direction gradually throughout a period of time. This is where they evolved out of one way of life and into something else due to getting all they could from their previous belief system. They might have received a moment of clarity where their current belief system was no longer making sense to them. Those around them will be able to examine their trajectory and point out that the person was showing early signs of this change before they transformed. It might seem over night to some, but in truth the shift is a gradual process.

What many of the law of attraction and abundance products do that is good is that it helps you get motivated and take responsibility for your life. It helps you get your mindset into that of winning. If you don't have that problem, then it'll probably do little for you except to give you positive reminders and tips. For someone perpetually stuck, miserable, or stagnant, then it can help them incorporate positive insights and steps to take to believe in themselves enough to do something about their life in the areas they are able to.

There are also those that are stuck so deep in

that abyss of pessimism and disappointment that it can take more work to climb out of that and start to feel good about what you can do to change things. Some of them end up despising all of this positive thinking and feel good talk that they fault the people that genuinely reside in a happy space. Blaming them for your unhappiness isn't going to change anything. It will ensure you remain stuck in that darkness.

I have reached that wall of disappointment and frustration too. Those moments were rare and would flush in and out. I was always able to bring God back up within me not long afterwards. This helped me get back on track again and to make positive successful changes in my life.

You know what works for you and what doesn't. If the law of attraction philosophies seem bogus and don't work for you, then partake in something that does work for you. Although, the odds of someone being anti-law of attraction reading a book like this one would be highly unlikely. They may look at the colorful cover and say, "Hogwash, just another abundance book in an oversaturated market as it is. Money peddler."

If I were in this for the money, then I would've become a banker, broker, or investor, not a creative artist, which I've been since I was a child able to pick up a pen.

Some explain that the like attracts like theory isn't accurate, when that's not typically the case. Take a look at how many people around the planet are gossips, angry, and always complaining, then examine the friendships around them as well as their lives. The odds are those friends are similar to them, with their lives riddled with drama and disappointment. This is because it is unlikely that someone who is anti-gossip would be hanging out with someone that is a gossip. This is part of what it means when someone says that like attracts like.

Notice the kind of life those that are negative live. You may notice that the person seems to have to endure one gigantic hurdle after another. While another more positive smiling person seems to have it easier. Since everyone and everything is made up of energy matter, and energy spreads, then it is feasible to understand that energy can bring in more of the same essence to that person. Making daily changes in your life that are on the positive side will have a positive effect on the kind of life you're living over time.

People easily become influenced by the people they hang around with. One example case scenario might be where a Straight-A student that is together, poised, and always doing the right thing starts to hang out with peers who are not like that. Those peers smoke cigarettes, drink alcohol, and do drugs at a young age. Suddenly the Straight-A impressionable student falls down the path of drug and alcohol addiction due to hanging with this new group.

Some might find the law of attraction to be a placebo effect. This is where you pop a pill believing it will give you a positive well-being state you're looking to achieve, and consequently you move into that state by the will of your thoughts. When in truth the pill may be doing nothing, but your mind has convinced you that you are in that state because you took that pill that claims to achieve certain affects. Does it matter if it's a placebo effect if it's positively working for you?

That's an example of believing something you've taken is working, when the truth is it may be your mind that has convinced you that it's working when you never truly needed it. This is how powerful the mind is. It can convince you something works or doesn't work.

If the law of attracting abundance is a placebo effect that helps someone attract in abundance, then who is someone to judge if the person experiencing that is accomplishing what they desired by incorporating the law of attraction tools into their life. Who cares how they do it if they are reaching the destination they wanted to. There is also no tangible proof to be provided that this same person would accomplish the exact same success without knowing about the law of attraction principles. There are people that don't buy the law of attraction principles and become successful. They had incorporated the law of attraction principles without realizing they did or knowing what those principles are.

When the law of attraction hasn't worked for someone, the automatic response is to attempt to debunk it and call it bogus. Attempting to disprove something because it did not work for you does not necessarily mean it doesn't work. It just didn't work for that particular person. It's the same way some have said they prayed for something, but nothing came to be, so they stop believing there is more out there beyond this planet. That also doesn't mean there isn't or that there is. It just means that one particular person did not get a prayer request answered.

Statistically there are a higher percentage number of people around the world that believe in the power of prayer over not praying. There are also a great many people that did not believe in the attracting in abundance philosophies, until they started to see tangible results.

As a thinking, feeling, conscious being, you are contemplating and computing everything around you and how that relates to your own reality. You are deciding based on evidence or lack of whether or not something can have some measure of truth in it. This sparks up healthy debates between those who believe and those who do not.

Once a debater gets into attacking another person, then they are making their point null and void. Resorting to name calling because someone's view is different than yours with something is no longer debate, but totalitarian. You've then moved into the space of being unable to communicate efficiently and intellectually with compassion, rather than aggressively bulldozing over someone angrily because they won't bend to your point of view.

The law of attraction is intention based which cannot be measured scientifically. The human intellect and brain are more powerful than one realizes. Your thoughts and emotions are more powerful than you realize. This all has the immense power to create a different reality. This is how the universal planet has evolved in its respective places to date. It started out with humanities intention to believe they would change something in their powerful minds, then they took action to make it happen and the change was made. This is regardless if another person agreed or disagreed with a particular change happening. It was essentially carried out under the universal laws of attraction.

Another misunderstanding of the law of attraction is that it allegedly purports to claim that if something bad has happened to someone, then it more than likely happened because of their negative thoughts. While it is true to an extent, it is not true in every single case.

I can personally recall those times in my life in the past when my mind was racing with negativity, depression, and bad anxiety that without a doubt one negative challenging thing after another began to take place. There was no way that I could not be conscious enough to deny the pattern. As soon as I calmed down with the racing negative thoughts, suddenly circumstances started to level out and calm down. I have experienced and witnessed that with myself, and with others way too many times to not notice the pattern.

Therefore, to one extent every soul's reality is being perpetuated in a certain way by their own doing in their mind. There are circumstances that you're born into that are more challenging than someone else's for various reasons, but that doesn't mean you asked for it or are destined to that. A great many people have successfully changed their circumstances through the power of their mind, positive intention, thinking, feeling, and action.

There are also isolated circumstances where someone was high on life and everything had been going great for so long, then a major catastrophe hits them. This doesn't mean they asked for it or that they drew that to them. There are circumstances in life that happen for people that have nothing to do with the law of attraction. There are circumstances that were created at the hands of someone else's free will choice that had a snowball effect where it hit you too. You are not invincible because you follow the laws of attraction when it comes to behavior, thoughts, and feelings. No one is exempt from challenges on Earth.

The deeper meaning of the laws of attracting in abundance is to motivate the stagnant soul into forward motion towards their dreams. Rise up, stand up, know what you want, hone in on it, and start figuring out ways that you will obtain it, then take that first action step towards it.

One of the main purposes of the laws of attraction and abundance is that people need to be motivated and feel empowered. This is why millions of people are drawn to the teachings of the law of attracting in abundance. Because people want to accomplish things and have their dreams come true. They're here living an Earthly life likely living existences that are dull in jobs they don't care about just to survive physically. As long as they're here they figure, "I may as well try to do what I love."

The spiritual teachings by various spiritual empowerment teachers, authors, speakers helps in giving them the tools and motivation to go after their dreams. Those that deflate the teachings or find it to be false either didn't gain anything from it, life dealt them a poor hand, it's against their religion of choice, or they're just negative curmudgeons drudging through life miserably. Who wants to be around any of that anyway. They may also be unlikely to be motivated by much. This is the current existence they're choosing. Don't knock those who feel empowered by the metaphysical spiritual empowerment teachings of others. Not all of those teachers are in it for the money or are even making all that much to begin with. They just enjoy the work.

People live different lives from one another. Everyone is having a different soul reality from another person. They all will not have the exact same experiences as someone else. You could be sitting next to the same colleague for months or years, yet you're both experiencing different realities and perceptions, but still finding a common ground to be civil enough to get along swimmingly.

While my Spirit team can only discuss things in terms of generalities rather then specifics, the truth is specific cases exist for every one of the billions of souls on the planet screaming and fighting for attention and gifts from Heaven. Human nature can be called a barbaric entitled seeking bunch, but that is the nature of Earth's reality. Everyone has an opinion and everyone thinks everyone else's opinion is invalid compared to their own. Deep down in many of those souls is a good person at heart who can manifest magical abundance manifestations through the power of their own mind. You can will it for good or evil, blessings or challenges, so choose wisely since both have repercussions and miracles embedded within each.

CHAPTER NINE

Taking Action on Divine Guidance

You've done the visualization exercises, the dream boards, prayed and asked for help, yet nothing has moved in your life or has been forthcoming. Take a step back for a moment and look at any repetitive ideas that may have continuously entered your mind urging you to take action on. What repetitive feelings or thoughts have been hitting you, but you've brushed it aside, ignored it, or not followed it. This process requires your intuitive powers to determine whether the action step you keep getting is one generated from your ego or is Divinely guided.

Generally, a Divinely guided idea or action step will come in several times or more, whereas something from your ego may come in an inconsistent way. A Divine impression that sifts into your soul would be an idea that harms no one, including yourself, on any level whether emotionally, physically, mentally or spiritually.

Ideas that are manufactured from the ego would be things like get rich quick schemes or a longing for public notoriety, popularity, or fame. Fame is usually just a side effect that happens out of one's talent or gifts, but it's not something the talented person seeks out. They just want to be able to participate in work they love. Any fame or fortune that enters the picture is a side effect of diving into that passion, but it is one that the talented person could do without as long as they can do their work without fear of not having enough money to pay their bills.

Your Spirit team steps in to assist you while on your journey. They guide you towards particular accomplishments at the right time. They could be helping you with a specific issue indefinitely for awhile, sometimes daily, but then there are times where they step back and allow you to make the free will choice. They can't live your life for you and make every single shred of decision making. You would never learn anything or experience life if they were continuously making all of your choices for you. Since most people don't typically listen to other people, it's unlikely they would listen to their

Spirit team.

They may guide you by getting you to notice someone or something that can help you achieve a particular desire. It could be by implanting the information into your consciousness where you can sense you're supposed to take action on something. They will continue to offer the same action step indefinitely until you finally take it. It doesn't matter if one week passes or one year. That same action step will be put in front of you until it's taken. Once you've taken action on that step, then they will show you the next step, and so forth.

When it comes to matters of love, they will put particular soul mate choices in your path intended to connect with you, but then it is up to you and/or this other person to notice it and act on it. They work with the other person's guides to guide that person toward you, while your own guides are guiding you towards them. That's quite a bit of guiding going on behind the scenes in hopes that both parties notice. They'll get you in the room alone together to face each other, but then it's up to the both of you to do the rest of the work. If neither of you do, then it's back to the drawing board for both sets of guides to continuously work to orchestrate the meeting again and again in hopes that action will be taken. This can only go on for so long before the moment passes and neither is unable to keep the orchestration from happening. At that point a lost opportunity has passed for both parties.

Perhaps you have fear about taking that step, or you don't know how you'll do it, or you've already tried that but it didn't work. The idea is still coming in trying to get you to notice it for a reason. Don't discredit those ideas that require you to take action. Taking action is another key step to opening the floodgates of abundance.

Act on the continuing positive nudges you receive and follow it. Don't allow worry or fear to set in blocking you from moving forward. Avoid inviting in more of that negative worry stuff to you. Some people choose to create a vision board, images, or positive words posted around them that remind them of what they want. This assists in implanting the ideas into your mind, which will help direct the energy towards making something happen. The goal is to fill your life with positive words and phrases that are aligned with abundance.

Affirm only what you desire and not what is lacking or missing in your life. The more you affirm what you don't want, then the more likely you will bring in that which you don't want into your life. Since that's the case, you may as well work on affirming positive thoughts and feelings. It's easy to live in negativity since that's what the ego drives each soul to reside in. No one is exempt from the ego taking over and talking you out of positivity.

If you perpetually keep displaying negative thoughts and feelings, then changing that process will take daily practice to re-train your mind to think differently. Don't feel discouraged if you find that you keep reverting back to negativity or that it becomes difficult. Notice when the negativity comes in, pay attention to when that happens, and shift the energy into positive thoughts and feelings. It may take you months as you implement this new mindset into more optimism than pessimism. Practice altering your thoughts and feelings to positive ones. Being mindful and aware of when you fall into a negative pattern can accomplish this.

Pay Attention
To Divine Guidance

Maybe an action step you're guided to make is taking you out of your comfort zone. You're afraid of making a drastic move that you know deep down you desperately want to make, but you're fearful of what will or will not come if you take action. Trust the continuous guidance your Spirit team is giving you. This is putting your faith and trust in God and the Universe that there is a Divine plan laid out to assist you.

At the same time, you want to be realistic and practical, such as you want to be careful walking away from a job when you don't have another one lined up. There are a great many success stories that include someone taking a huge risk by walking away from a job before they found another. Still you want to move cautiously with that kind of a major decision.

A reader named John owns an art gallery selling expensive art to high end clients. Before he was doing that, he was a salesperson for a company. He would work from home most of the time, but wasn't putting in much of an effort as a salesperson. His heart wasn't in it, so instead he dabbled around with this art selling idea. Eventually the company he was a salesperson at let him go when they discovered he wasn't putting in any effort. After he was let go, he dove head on into his work as an art dealer. He opened his gallery and ended up attracting in all sorts of clients and buyers that his side business started booming. He now owns his this successful business. He was also able to buy his own home and he's never been happier.

The way he told me the story had struck a chord, as I've listened to other similar stories. Sometimes getting fired, laid off, or quitting is the severe push one needs to completely focus on their side business and making it a full time money making business. It's true that it can be risky doing it that way, but many have been successful at that. They're no longer being weighed down by this day job that drops their vibration making them miserable. That state is not helpful in building your side business.

When they were let go from the day job, this put them into high gear where they kicked up the action efforts into their side business. They had a bit of a financial cushion to give themselves a few months to dive into building this side business without fear of not being able to pay their bills. In John's case, he was able to increase the income as an art dealer to the point that looking for another day job was no longer necessary. This isn't advising you to quit your job if that's a concern. Always move cautiously with big decisions weighing the pros and cons before acting.

Maybe your Spirit team continues to nudge you to apply for a job you always wanted, but you had already applied at that same place a year prior and received no response. Months or a year later the job is still on your mind. Many companies are open to people re-applying or re-submitting their resume or credentials every six months. You may have received no response the first time, but the repetitive Spirit guidance coming in on it again may be no accident. You're being asked to try again, as they see the timing is now right. Your name also becomes more familiar to the employer that does the hiring. They are more likely to call a familiar name to come in for an interview over a name they don't know.

This same scenario has been true for me. As far as with the jobs I've had in the past from the record store to the film business. I was turned down initially or I received no response from them. I tried on several occasions on a later date and received no response or a, "Sorry we're not hiring right now". I tried again at a much later date and that was when I struck gold. This time I received a response to come in, met with them, and was hired on the spot. Imagine if I didn't follow the hunches to try again.

Perhaps you were turned down or you turned them down, but the hunches kept coming in stronger over time, so you try again. It's the trying again part in the equation when it all comes together.

Sometimes you're supposed to be at a specific job at a time in your life for a reason that might not be understood while it's in motion. You may be longing to quit this day job for some time and cannot understand what the delay is. You could be gaining skills at this day job that you will be utilizing later. You may not think so at the time you are working the job. It's only in the future when you're at the next gig or chapter in your life that you look back and realize why you were there for the time that you were. This concept goes for relationships of all types from friendships, business, to love as well too.

You could be single and constantly bumping into the same person in passing or while out and about getting you both to notice one another. You and this person may secretly be developing a crush on one another that you start to pick up on with the mutual warm smiles and *hello-how are you's*. As time progresses you both gain confidence to say more than hello and strike up longer conversations. This is how I've met some of the ones I ended up with in long term love relationships with in the past.

There are times where you've been psychically blocked or you're not receiving a crystal-clear Divine answer on something, while other times it will slam into your consciousness in a matter of seconds. For those times where nothing is coming in, it helps to pray, connect with God, ask for intervention, signs, messages, and guidance. Ask your Spirit team to help you notice what these messages could be.

Before bed and drifting off to sleep, ask your Spirit team to come into your dreams and communicate with you there. Your ego is asleep and your consciousness rises leaving you more receptive and open to receiving the Divine content while in a dream state. Ask that they help you remember the dream, because sometimes the dreams can be so vivid, but the second you wake up it's gone and vanished. Keep a journal or notepad within reach while asleep so that when you wake up, you can quickly jot down the images you received in the dream as soon as possible before it's gone. Even if it has no meaning to you at that point. Jot it down as it could have significance later.

Dreaming is also connected to Clairvoyance, which is known as clear seeing or clear viewing. Many that have vivid dreams regularly tend to have strong Clairvoyance. Clairvoyance requires some decoding on your part, since the messages come in as visuals that are more symbolic than a direct message. Write down everything you remember seeing in the dream, even if it was a color. Colors have symbolic meanings as well too. There could be some important clues in your dreams that were planted into your subconscious to help you.

CHAPTER TEN

Working to Find Meaning in Your Life

Working in a job or career that has deep meaning and fulfillment to you while getting paid for it is something many want to achieve. It can be frustrating when you're an intelligent thinking talented consciousness who has dreams of wanting to partake in work that means something to you, while being efficiently compensated enough to survive. You find you're stuck in a life soul crushing job that you head off to day after day simply for the paycheck.

In the film, *Riding in Cars with Boys*, the Drew Barrymore character made a statement in it that forever stuck, *"I still haven't accepted that this is my life. I wish I could be dumb and then I wouldn't know better. And I could be happy and stop hoping."*

Her character was driven and intelligent. She was trying to work on her passion and get paid for it, but was constantly struggling against the flow with one roadblock after another rising up. It felt as if she was wasting her time in life. She figured if she wasn't bright, then longing for something greater than what she currently had, and fighting to make her dreams happen wouldn't be on her radar. If she was indifferent or naïve, then she'd be perfectly content working at jobs that didn't matter to her. She wouldn't feel miserable spending her days wishing and hoping for a blessing. She does achieve what she wished and desired for, but it wasn't without the struggle, longing, faith, and action steps taken.

Career transitions are challenging for anyone, because transitions in general are life altering and require effort. Many self-employed entrepreneur success stories also discuss how difficult it can be at first. A Medium friend of mine started out working a day job she hated in New York City. She kept the psychic part of herself quiet at work to avoid ridicule. Reaching the breaking point, she had $10,000 saved and used that to move out to Venice, California. The money quickly left her with the move itself. This resulted in her having to live out of her car. Eventually, that all turned around with continued faith, prayer, and action. She now has a successful psychic practice and her own home, but it was not without its initial struggles where she almost gave up.

I've always been a huge fan of rags to riches success stories since I was a kid. Those are the stories that reveal someone who came from nothing and made something out of their life. They weren't born into money and nor did they have a well to do life. Instead they had to work harder than those who were born into money or had stuff handed to them. They had the struggles where it seemed impossible, but they soon climbed the ranks to the top. Those are the inspiring stories that remind you that anyone can do it if they believe and try hard enough.

This isn't necessarily about accumulating financial riches, which is a hollow superficial goal. This is about being able to turn your life purpose, hobby, or passion into a career where you are making enough money that you no longer have to work at jobs you despise just for the paycheck.

Rags to riches stories often entail someone who just wanted to be able to do work that was their passion. They weren't looking to make a million dollars. The financial abundance that came flowing in was a positive side effect to them putting effort into their passion. They put in positive energy that came in naturally because they were enjoying the work. This attracted in the financial abundance.

When you feel no guidance or messages coming in from above, then it could be that you're experiencing a block. This is why raising your vibration is another important factor, because doing that helps in dissolving any blocks. One way to raise your vibration is through exercise and working out. This assists you in being a clearer vessel with the Divine, not to mention the health benefits you receive out of that too. I wrote the first *Raising Your Vibration* book if you desire additional information surrounding this particular topic.

I've also forever been a strong advocate for exercise since I was a kid. Since my teen years, I've been into exercise, working out, and taking care of myself as much as possible. I'll go hiking in the mountains, to rock climbing in the desert, to regular jogs and biking on the beach where I'll hang out for hours connecting with Spirit. This is because exercise awakens every cell in your body and soul, but so does being in nature. When you're exercising in nature, then that's a double whammy that assists in raising your vibration. Those cells that are awakened are transporters that communicate with spirit beings from beyond. When those cells awaken, then the information flows in more effortlessly. Exercise does a body good releasing happy endorphin chemicals. Happiness lifts your vibration cracking open the Divine communication line.

Getting into a happy state, exercising, and being in nature will all help raise your vibration. When you combine all three at once, then what a powerhouse feeling that is. A raised vibration is what acts as a funnel for your Spirit team to communicate with you much more easily. It also brings in free flowing good stuff into your world. Forcing happiness or pretending to be happy won't work, so it will have to be authentic joy.

Exercise has always been like oxygen to me. The initial getting to the exercise may be tough for some, but once you get into some form of cardio to get the body warmed up, then this gets the oxygen working through your cells. It feels like soaring above the clouds making you feel good.

FEAR – THE ABUNDANCE BLOCK

There's nothing more paralyzing and detrimental to human beings than fear. Fear has plagued humankind since they first started inhabiting Earth. Fear blocks you from moving forward and prevents the positive flow of abundance. Fear can come in the disguise of worry, stress, depression, and anger. It will expand negative emotions and create madness depending on the case. For instance, hate crimes against someone who is different than the antagonist generally begins to breed in the womb of fear. The antagonist might respond by saying, "I'm not afraid of them. I just don't like them."

Basically, they don't like anyone that falls into a particular demographic. This comes from a subconscious fear of coming across someone who isn't exactly like you. God throws everyone together on the same rock to learn tolerance, acceptance, and forgiveness. Those are some of the most difficult traits that people have trouble with conveying.

More people than not used to have hatred

towards anyone who had a same sex attraction. Once they realized that every other person they loved around them fit that description, they gradually changed their tune realizing they made a mistake about their hatred, and just didn't know any better. Now it's becoming increasingly common and accepted, but there are still those living in the stone ages with a limited view who have yet to gain love for those not like them. Using Biblical text that was added in at a later date by superstitious fearful men isn't a good excuse, since God created all breathing life this way for a reason. God doesn't have hang ups about two souls in love with each other regardless of their gender. Love is what He desires to see, so in that instant when two souls are in love, He is pleased. In fact, God has disdain for those that express hatred over two souls in a committed love relationship. Jesus Christ was the same way. His complaint was over adultery and not about committed love between two souls.

Dive down deep as to why you don't like someone. Hating an entire group isn't valid because there are good and bad people in all groups. When you pull one person out of that group you despise and you're locked in a room with them to have a conversation, there is a greater chance that when you both leave that room you'll like them. If anything, you will both at least have a bit more compassion, respect, and understanding of them. The only way that will never work is if someone's consciousness is not raised. A limited consciousness permanently resides in darkness unable to break free. The darkness is where fear lives.

I've conducted social experiments with this as well. This is where I've placed two people in a room together who are in opposition on the political spectrum. The intention of putting them in the room together was to get them to have friendly conversation outside of their personal political choices. Nine times out of ten they generally ended up liking each other or at least respecting each other despite their personal political values. When you take the time to get to know someone who is different from you, then eventually you come to a greater more compassionate understanding of that person.

You've likely witnessed people attacking another person over their personal views. This does nothing to change that person. Seeking to understand them and have a cordial sit down conversation with them is more likely to gain some measure of respect. This is not always the case amongst those rare exceptions, but in many paradigms it is. If you already know they can't be reasoned with, then walk away.

How does this all apply to manifesting abundance? Fear energy is one of the major culprits to blocking the flow of positive abundance. It doesn't matter if the fear is over achieving your goals or fear that causes you to despise an entire group of people. It is still fear energy in the eyes of the Universe. Fear lives within the darkness of a soul's ego. Fear is responsible for the chaos energy that forever surrounds the planet when humankind is operating from a low vibration. Fear will make you doubt yourself and bring on baseless worry energy.

Doubts and worry that you will not achieve or succeed what you desire stems from fear. When that happens, then you need a healthy dose of inspiration that can be found in empowering music, books, or films. This is one of the positives of entertainment, which was created to help people forget about their troubles, help them to lighten up, or give them a dose of inspiration. Balanced entertainers who remain neutral on their personal values while in the public eye don't always get enough credit for this goal at times.

The alternative rock song, *High Hopes*, by Panic at the Disco sings, *"I had to have high hopes for a living. Shooting for the stars when I couldn't make a killing. Didn't have a dime, but I always had a vision. Didn't know how, but I always had a feeling I was going to be that one in a million."*

Listen to empowering music with positive lyrics that help motivate you. Watch movies about those who came from nothing and made something with their life. Rags to riches stories can be incredibly inspiring. People that had nothing and struggled with little to no money, but soon overcame that and made something with their life. They might be films like *Erin Brockovich, People Vs. Larry Flynt,* or *Joy.*

Many successful known entertainers admit to having self-doubts or fear, which humanizes them and helps them to be relatable to their audience. They fear they're not that good, or that they'll be found out that they're no good. They are good at what they do, they are popular, and at the top of their game, but they're also human and have human emotions that their success is a fluke.

It helps to have some perspective that everyone experiences doubts or worries, but don't let that cripple you to the point of non-movement. You rise above it and keep forging forward making the most of what you can do while you are here. You may as well try, because what else do you have to lose?

DISPLAY OPTIMISM AND GRATITUDE

It took me a long time to move away from relying on regular day jobs to pay me and realize the income was ultimately coming from God. You could do your life purpose work if the financial support part of it is given to God to pay you. You develop less worry and guilt, and more faith and optimism knowing that you're taken care of when you modify your thinking process. This is by changing your perspective to understand that God is ultimately your source of income. This is rather than heavily focusing on a company or a boss to rely on to stay afloat and be taken care of. It takes a great leap of faith to be able to let go of that control. Jobs come and go, but God is always constant. Your reality in response to that might be, "That's all great, but the checks are written to me by the company I work for. They don't say God on them as the payee."

Ultimately all forms of abundance are trickling down from God, to the company, and to you. It's no accident that you're at a particular job. If fear or worry enters your mind, then alter the sentence to something positive. *"God, thank you so much for your help with this. Thank you for the blessings you've bestowed on me to date. Thank you also for ensuring I have a place to live without fear or worry that my bills won't get paid. Thank you for my strong health and happiness."*

A huge lift inside can be felt when changing your sentences from something challenging and negative to something aligned with gratitude, optimism, and faith. When you heavily complain about things never going your way, then this creates a huge heavy burden on your soul while bringing more of that into your life.

Worry creates more worry, while joy creates more joy. When you feel like your job is not going as planned or you hate it, and your mind constantly goes there whenever you have a free minute, then take a step back and halt the tone of that thinking. Shift those words to ones of gratitude. Think of the good things you have in your life. The ones that would make your life worse if you didn't have those good things. They can be items such as your car that is in good condition helping you get to and from work without worry. You don't worry much about your car until something goes wrong with it, then you realize how grateful you are to have a car that runs. Don't wait for something bad to happen to realize what you have, but be grateful now.

It's easy to take things for granted until those

blessings unacknowledged are taken away. When you are in a negative space, then stop and direct your attention to the blessings you do have.

Maybe you've reached the point of feeling sorry for yourself. You find that you say things like, "Why does everyone else get the good stuff, but I'm still struggling to get my share of the blessings?"

The same ones feeling sorry for themselves regularly will also moan about not having any friends. When you look closer, you notice they seem to be surrounded by numerous people who fit the description of a friend. They're still unhappy and despondent not seeing it because perhaps they have conditions on what they expect from a friend. You can have a pity party begging for attention from others, or you can get over it and continue persevering on doing what you're called to do. Never beg for anyone's friendship and attention.

One of the general meanings of the *Four of Cups* card in the *Tarot* will at times reveal someone feeling sorry for themselves as if what they want will never come. They sit next to one cup tipped over with their head down disappointed. The card symbolism also shows three cups filled with blessings behind that person, but they're not seeing those gifts. Pay attention to the blessings existing in your present moment. One often looks at what they don't have, rather than what they currently do. Acknowledging and displaying gratitude for what you have now is a positive abundance attractor.

CHAPTER ELEVEN

Empower Your Soul

Signs and symbols of angelic help is all around when you take the time to pay attention and notice it. An important step is to ask for help, since no being in Heaven can intervene or offer assistance for anyone who doesn't ask for help. Some people may not believe that's possible, or they have stopped believing, so they continue to suffer. It doesn't take much effort or time out of your day to stop what you're doing and ask for assistance from above. What do you have to lose by asking? If nothing else you've tried has helped, then what could it hurt to say the words?

Another step beyond asking for help is to be aware by paying attention to the repetitive action steps you may be guided to do. You might say, "I've asked for help and heard nothing."

Sometimes you're not going to hear the answer audibly or verbally. You might be given messages, answers, and guidance through nudges, signs, symbols, or other ways that can get your attention. Perhaps after you've asked for help, you're invited to an event or party, but choose not to go because you're uncomfortable with social settings. You failed to notice the synchronicity that took place following you asking for heavenly guidance. Your Spirit team may have been orchestrating a meeting between you and another person who will be at this event. This other person could end up being someone that is connected to a future job you'll have or they could be the next relationship partner. Instead you chose to stay home alone when you were being asked to follow this guidance with an action step.

Asking for help also entails asking another person for help. You might be afraid to ask someone for assistance because you're shy or you don't want to bother or burden them. You might have a great deal of pride and are used to doing things yourself. Even the most self-sufficient person can use a hand occasionally. Sometimes the support can come in the form of helpful words of advice from another person. If you're down and out, just talking to someone can be a great way to access support.

You might ask for Divine assistance, but then

you start visualizing how you expect the answer to come in. The visualization soon forms into worry, which is a prayer killer. When you ask for help, step out of the way and busy yourself with other things. Meanwhile, allow the prayer request to come into your life the way it's supposed to on Divine timing. This is the same way you ask a friend or anyone else for help with something, but then you end up getting frustrated. You then take over and do it yourself, instead of allowing and trusting the other person to handle it in their own way. When you ask for Divine guidance or assistance, then let it go and step out of the way without interfering so God can handle it.

You could feel guilt or unworthiness about achieving success, which also creates a block. You see other successful people and the lower self part of you brings you down, "I'm nothing like them. Look at this woman. She's so good looking and this is why everyone is buying her products. And look at me, I don't have that look that people are attracted to."

Everyone has something of value to offer the public that helps them in some way. Looks will only get someone so far. Eventually looks fade, so if they don't have something else going for them, then they'll end up being a flash in the pan. Many have found this out the hard way. They were bowed down to for their looks in their twenties, but when they move into their thirties, forties, and beyond, they notice people are paying less attention to them. They discover society shuns or ignores them the way some do with older people on the sidewalk or in passing.

Negativity on any level can block you from achieving. Every soul is deserving of good on the planet, and every single person has something positive to offer. In higher spiritual truth, no one is more special than anyone else or below or above another, because all souls were made equally. Some souls have an easier time at evolving their consciousness than others. While other souls remain at one level throughout one Earthly lifetime.

In Heaven, all souls are considered one united. This is how it is supposed to be on Earth, even though the human ego convinces some people that they're either better or worse than another. It can be seen this way when you compare a giving Saint to a terrorist killer. In that comparison the differences are wide, but this is about both of those people's souls deep down at the core. When the soul is born into an Earthly life it is born with the highest God like qualities available and imaginable. It is only as the soul moves through its human journey do the experiences it endures shape and mold them to something else entirely.

The Godly traits the soul is born with are always inside them and forever accessible. The soul has to figure it out for itself and do the work to bring it back out again. As you're likely aware, not many accept that challenge and they end up suffering. Remembering your soul's true heritage makes you a powerful abundance attractor.

You are just as deserving of blessings, abundance, and success as any other soul being is. There is enough room on the planet for every single soul to experience success. There is always enough to go around. Everyone does and says things in their own way, therefore they all have the ability to showcase their unique talents in their distinctive way.

You go to a spiritual empowerment event to listen to five different guest speakers on motivation. They are all enjoyable talking about the same goal and content. They're each discussing it in their own way. This shows how everyone has something to offer surrounding the same topic, because not everyone says things in the same way. One speaker might not interest you, but they will interest someone else. The same goes for anyone in any field. One rock singer is different from another and appeals to the same or a different audience. There is enough room for everyone to contribute their talents in their own authentic and original way.

In today's world post technology, having access to the internet has given many talented people various opportunities to showcase their talents had they had not access to get online. Many businesses have closed up physical stores, but kept their business thriving through online sales. Many have been moving into starting up their own successful self-employment business.

There was this motivational YouTube video of this 18-year-old guy who was selling enough product online that he could do that full time. He explained that he doesn't have to take a full time 9-6 corporate office day job that he'll end up despising because he does so well with this internet business.

Sometimes he walks along the beach on a Tuesday afternoon when no one is there because they're all at their soul crushing corporate day jobs. He loves that freedom of space to clear his mind without the crowds. He's able to do that because he sets his own hours and makes enough where he can afford to do that. He's not a millionaire or rich by any means, but he makes enough consistently and regularly to pay his rent and bills without worry. It gives him the luxury of working when he wants to, rather than the rigid inflexible 9a-6p schedule that is the current norm. He gets more done in little time than it takes someone else in a corporate job. He also controls when he chooses to work.

There are many people moving into successful self-employment businesses today more than ever before. They started out by supplementing their income by taking a side day job. You just want to do your best to look for a day job that makes you smile enough to not feel stressed and worried, otherwise that energy will carry over to the side hobby you've been working at building.

COMPLAINING INTO ABUNDANCE

There is the reality that you may not have a choice and will have to accept any day job that comes your way. This is part of physical survival on Earth. You have to do what you need to do in order to stay afloat without worry.

During my day job tenure, I accepted any old job that I wasn't all that happy with, but they did give me some measure of flexibility. It was close to home and the safety net of that job enabled me to find an even better job that I truly wanted six months later.

When you feel worry and stress over your day job, or not having enough money to work on your life purpose, then you risk moving into complaining territory. Complaining is an abundance killer. If you spend your life complaining, you will guarantee that you will be given more to complain about.

Several of my friends and I have a pact where we step in if we see someone falling into perpetual complaining. This is pointed out to help one another stop the runaway train downwards. This is not done insensitively or to quiet ones voice from expressing itself. It also doesn't mean ignoring a problem one is experiencing. This is about taking a step back to evaluate what can be done about the issue that is causing the person to complain for days, weeks, and sometimes months.

When you are fearful about not finding a job, it will cause you to vent and complain about that. This isn't telling you to suppress your worries and fears, but rather get to the level of realizing when it's happening, have your quick complaint about it, but then shift that into something positive like an action step that can be done to help move out of that dirty cycle of complaining.

When I've prayed or asked for Divine assistance, then that was when the assistance eventually came. I wouldn't force-feed you prayer if it never worked for me. I'm also not insisting that anyone pray, except to say that prayer has always worked for me, otherwise I wouldn't do it. You might be a non-believer, but you are praying without realizing it. When your thoughts move into a plea or gratitude, then you've moved into prayer. You might call it an affirmation or just something you were thinking about, but it is a prayer that the Universe and Heaven are hearing come out of you. They will also hear you when you're incessantly complaining whether out loud or to anyone listening. Complaining that nothing is happening or changing for you will not suddenly bring in the blessings.

Complaining your way into abundance will not result in success. If you're going to continue complaining about something, then don't bother praying for it since the complaint will negate the prayer anyway. You ask for heavenly help, but nothing comes around as quick as you'd like it if at all, so you assume you've been given up on. You might play the victim card that no one was able to help, you're being ignored, and woe is me. You're trained to stand tall, pull yourself up by your bootstraps, and forge forward fearlessly with faith as your anchor.

Lean on your Spirit team for assistance when your faith and well-being are wavering. Work on being grateful for the blessings they've helped you with to date. Do you have clothes, food, and a roof over your head? Then say, "Thank you."

God or any enlightened being around you is not Santa Claus longing to drop gifts in your lap the second you ask for it. Some people are under the impression that the job of heavenly helpers is to grant your desires like a genie in a bottle. When that doesn't happen you automatically assume they must not exist or you're being ignored. You're expected to do the work yourself. Sitting around on your couch drinking a beer all day watching a sports game hoping gifts will fall from the ceiling onto your sofa is never going to happen. It's also not Heaven's job or anyone else's job to constantly tell you what to do, where to go, and when to do it. It's your job to do those things. You're given what you need, not necessarily what you want. Needs are the essentials such as housing, food, and clothing.

Spirit guides will step in when necessary to nudge you to move in a certain direction where the most benefit for your soul's growth exists. They will not live your life for you. You're not a puppet on a string that they're controlling. They are like any good best friend who taps you on the shoulder to get you to notice something important, but it's not their burden to carry if you fail to detect it. They can put the same repetitive cues in front of you to get you to see something, but there's nothing more they can do if you're not paying attention to it. If you don't make moves and go after what you want, they are not going to do it for you. If you don't have the confidence to go after what you want, then confidence gaining skills is one of your life purposes to master. Avoiding an action step towards making something happen is something you must learn to overcome and master.

Complaining is surrounded with undesirable

energy that lowers your vibration. Negative anything will manifest into health-related concerns down the line. Sometimes you fall into perpetual daily complaining that you don't even realize you are doing that because it's become habitual.

If everything that comes out of you is toxic or a harsh assaulting judgment, then that energy will grow and manifest into more of the same. It marinates into the cells and pores of your physical, emotional, and spiritual body making you permanently one with it. You may know someone like that, and you know they're a challenging person to be around.

The largest culprits put that energy out into the Universe by posting words aligned with toxicity on their social media accounts. They're not aware that the darkness has enveloped them. Having an understanding that the person can no longer help it can offer some measure of light in how you navigate around someone like that. The best thing to do is avoid or ignore them as much as possible. This is unless absolutely necessary such as in the work place where you have no choice but to face them. Limit contact to work related dialogue in those instances. Being around someone who is perpetually negative and toxic will affect you, your energy, and vibration. This has an effect in attracting in abundance by negating the process from working in your favor.

This isn't to say there isn't anything to complain about. The most enlightened being is mumbling a harmless complaint to themselves on occasion. The difference is that they are aware of when it happens, and they shift that complaint into a positive action effortlessly. Evolving souls prefer to hang around people that complain less over the toxic complainer.

Day to day issues happen to everyone all around the planet. Some of it can be extreme enough to push you to vent. Even the nicest, sweetest, most compassionate soul complains. This isn't about that, but about being aware and conscious of when you fall into a dark pattern of daily repetitive complaining that it's become all that you are.

When you find that you've fallen into perpetual complaining that it's now annoying you, then work on turning that complaint into positive action steps. An action step can be choosing to stop complaining. It can be to look at what you're complaining about, and finding creative ways to resolve whatever it is you're complaining about. If it's something that is not realistic or possible to correct, then work on letting it go. Divert your focus towards positive beneficial activities to distract your mind from the negative, while adding what you desire to your prayer request.

CHAPTER TWELVE

Increasing Faith
to Accomplish, Achieve, and Persevere

*C*raving human interaction and social stimulation is something sought out by many, while other people prefer to function alone. When you have a strong connection with God and Spirit, then you never feel lonely. Loneliness is ultimately longing for a connection to fulfill you that can only truly be satisfied by God. To have a mutually reciprocated blissful love union with another person is to know God, because a soul's best qualities are parts of Him.

Since it's sometimes difficult for a human soul to have a connection with God, the ego part of one's self will crave love, attention, and admiration from other people. It's temporarily fulfilling because no one can ever fill that space within you except God. God in this case is not that cliché image of a man with a beard sitting on a chair in the sky. This is the image that non-believers tend to overuse, which has no basis in the reality of the massive energy force that created all that IS.

All souls desire some form of companionship with at least one person. Some people might disagree, but they do crave some form of a relationship based in love if even through a social circle of friends.

A businessman might say that he only cares about work and money, yet he is cut off from the Universe and the Divine. If he didn't have to get it from some source connected to another person, then he wouldn't crave it at all. He needs other people around him. If they weren't around and all people were taken away from him so that he could be completely alone, then it wouldn't be long before he begins to go crazy and start to miss that stimulation and crave another person.

In the films, *Passengers* and *Cast Away*, both show one person functioning alone for a long period of time. Eventually they start to go a little mad due to not having another person to engage with at some point.

If this businessman showed up on Earth to find no other people, then he wouldn't know what he was missing. Because there is no material distraction, he would be more in tune to the Heavens unable to hear anything else. This is how human beings progressed in the beginning of civilization. They paid attention to the Heavens and their Divine senses to guide them on how to naturally progress.

Eventually it expanded and exploded to the point of never ending distractions. The more this chaos rose up, the less Divinely connected human beings became. There is no way to escape that and not be aware that it's happening, even if you live in the middle of nowhere. While you might be more connected to Spirit in those areas, you lose the connection when you turn your television on, you surf the internet, you read media stories, or you hop on your phone. Now you are no longer spiritually connected.

You might be connected to one another through technological devices, but in a distant loveless way. You are not connected to God through those forms. The entire planet is unsettled making it near impossible to sense the Divine energy that way. Your subconscious is aware of it, even if you're not paying attention to it in the present moment. If you're a highly spiritually connected being, then you're versed and readily able to move in and out of the Spirit connection whenever it calls for it.

Your soul's life force dies little by little living a life you're unhappy with. Perhaps you feel emotionally dead as if you don't have much else to give anymore. You've asked for help for years, and became doubtful that it will ever happen at this point. You're waiting, hoping, praying, and taking action for years wondering if a miracle and blessings will reveal itself to you. It can make you doubt, lose faith, and question if there is a God. It sounds like a roller coaster ride of voices competing with one another from your ego to your angels, to your ego, to your angels.

I love films from all genres, from horror, to intense dramas, to Fratboy comedies, and to films with an uplifting spiritually based message like, *The Shack*.

In *The Shack*, the character Mack is a Man that grew up in a home full of physical and emotional abuse. As a Father in present day, one of his youngest daughters is abducted by a serial killer that rapes and kills her. Something this extreme and bleak had to take place so that viewers can understand how this man's faith and trust in God and life in general is just gone.

He endures emotional and mental anguish, horror, anger, and a loss of spirit. He's led to the Shack where his daughter was killed by who he believes is the killer. He's in for a powerful awakening when he discovers it's the Holy Trinity, but taking the form of people. Jesus and the Holy Spirit are there along with God Himself, who takes the form of a woman.

The man is confused and says to God, "Do I know you?"

God chuckles, "Not very well." And then with firm inviting comfort, "But we can work on that."

I loved the film from that point when the man gets to hang out and develop a stronger relationship with the Holy Trinity. They take the form of a warm cozy family that feels like a Hallmark card feeding you spiritual wisdom that isn't that far off from the truth. Through this relationship, they help this man regain his faith and hope in himself and life again.

Some strict religious people found this to be heresy, while some non-believers found it to be like a church sermon. As usual, I don't hang on either side and found *The Shack* to be uplifting, truthful, with a Universal message of love. It feels like taking a warm bath in the Paradise of Light with Heaven's greats that is moving, joyful and empowering.

FOCUS ON YOUR PURPOSE

When your consciousness is raised, it is not uncommon to feel disconnected from other people and view human life as trivial. This is when it's time to do an inventory check of how the months and years to date have gone for you. Examine your triumphs, sorrows, successes, and challenges. What was lost and what was gained throughout that time. You'd be surprised to find the hidden blessings you never thought much of until you look back on it. When things are going amazingly, people don't usually notice it as much as they do when things are going horribly. One can take it for granted until you take a moment to note, "Okay, my rent gets paid every month, my health is great, and I have a working car that gets me to my job."

Look forward to the coming time up ahead with

promise and hope. Believe that it will get better and accept nothing less than that. Celebrate your wins and accomplishments to acknowledge what you've done.

Success comes and goes the way fame comes and goes. One of the best dreams to come true is being able to turn your love and hobby into a financially lucrative career. You are closer than someone else might be if you understand the concept of manifestation and asking for what you want. If you're stressed out at your job regularly, is the job worth it? Make wise choices in your life that do not result in leaving you in a bind where you're perpetually unhappy. Take a job for less pay and live beneath your means, until you find the work that makes you feel bliss again.

Looking to the future with optimism you might sometimes find you've been chasing rainbows that evaporate as quickly as the champagne fizzles in your glass. You need not search long and hard for some measure of magic to reveal itself since it's always resided within you. You are loved even when you doubt it, avoid it, shun it and do everything in your power to deny it. When you reach that threshold of completing your Earthly run, the only thing you take with you is love. If you gain anything while here, then remember to love more, give more, and have compassion no matter how unpopular it is. Only then can you truly discover that magic you secretly desire.

Keep a journal for a month and write down every single thing that bothers you. This means a trending topic you found yourself falling into.

After enough time has passed, revert back to that journal to see what you wrote. Notice if it has truly had any positive effect on changing your life, or if it was just another time waster you fell emotionally drawn to, but could care less about months later. It will be mind boggling to witness the long list of time wasters that prevented you from being happy and moving forward.

Focus on your life purpose rather than time wasters that act as a procrastination technique to prevent you from getting to work on what you desire. The tiny action steps you make are creating change even if you don't feel like it is while in the midst of it. You may think that someone else will take care of an issue, but no one really is or does. If you need to go it alone, then you have to go it alone and tackle it one issue at a time. One small action step can get the energy flowing in that direction. Research and seek out ways that change can be made in the area of your interest that you strongly feel needs to be changed.

Sometimes healthy time wasters have good mind enhancing properties, such as those card games like Solitaire or emailing friends back to get you out of a procrastination cycle. You just want to make sure you don't fall too deep into the time wasters that you find four hours have passed and you have yet to get to work on your dreams. Even just a small amount of time working on action steps that can one day bring you what you desire will make all the difference in the world. It's definitely more advantageous than contributing nothing towards it.

CHAPTER THIRTEEN

Stuck in a Job
That Drains Your Life Force

Some believe that if you're given a gift, a particular talent, or a divinely inspired idea, then you should give it away without charging money for it. There's the romanticized old view of the starving artist pining away in a tin can, which is absurdly unrealistic. In today's age, unless you were born into money or you're living off a large trust fund, then if you want to survive you'll need to work to make money. You have to charge for your gifts and services. This is not out of greed, but in order for you to pay for rent, food, and clothing. When those basic practical necessities are taken care of, then you're able to focus on what you love without worry or concern of survival.

If you gave everything away for free, then you couldn't survive and would end up on the streets. You would have to find a super uncreative full time job on the side to pay your bills, but that would end up sapping your creative energy and life force needed to apply towards your ultimate passion and life purpose. Not all life purposes are financially gaining ones. The purposes that are not financially gaining ones, you may still want to find a money making job that excites you on some level that it doesn't feel like work.

There was a time people would barter and do a trade with someone for goods. You'd offer something of value to someone that can give you something of value such as food, clothing, housing, etc. Eventually that changed over the centuries where you would need money to purchase items. You can't go to the grocery store today and offer them a material item in exchange for food. This is partially why spiritual teachers charge for their services. The other reason is you need to have a balanced exchange of energy. You give someone money for goods or services. This exchange keeps the giving and receiving energy balanced.

The only spiritual teachers who don't charge are those who work in a church, but those are non-profit companies where they are receiving donations from members of the congregation to stay afloat. If they didn't receive donations, they would close up, and many of them have. That money goes into their paychecks and the upkeep of the church, so even they are charging essentially.

There are a great many talented healers and artists contributing positive work and efforts towards humanity and their life purpose, but sadly many of them are stuck in regular day jobs that suck up their time and energy. This makes it challenging to pursue their true passion and make a decent living out of it.

What makes that feeling worse is that an enormous amount of these day jobs pack on unnecessary stress that stalls you from forward movement, while lowering your morale and placing a heavy weight on your soul and well-being state. This is because those jobs are bathed in toxic energy in one person or more around them who are disconnected from spirit and the bigger universal picture.

If that's not the case and all are a pleasure to be around, the lowered morale can come from your lengthy commute to the job, or because the job is not your passion, takes up most of your time, and is gravely demanding on you on all levels. That alone can be the reason for the lowered morale. As an empath sensitive this can be exceptionally taxing on your system, but this is wearing on anyone regardless if they are in tune or not. Being aware of what's greater than your physical body makes it more depressing to be in Earthly set ups that bring you permanently down.

If you're in this kind of a situation, then you are aware that a high percentage of your time is connected to this day job on some level even when you're not at work. This can stall a talented person from working towards what they want to do with their life in the long run. They soon give up and lose faith believing that the Universe is working against them and that they're just not as lucky in the way that others are.

Don't give up on the account of someone else. It can be tough at times, but you have to keep going and fighting to do what you truly desire. Your lack of happiness in achieving is not a result of anything you did or did not do. It is not because the Universe favors someone else over you. Everyone has their own timeline towards that achievement. For some it might happen right away, while for others in can take years and for some even decades.

One guy informed me that when he's not at work he's sometimes having dreams at night that involves his place of employment or about his colleagues. It didn't start off that way, but when the feeling of wanting to do what he loved grew, then his hatred for his day job grew, which started to manifest into his dreams. This job is embedded deeply into his consciousness.

When you're asleep and having dreams about your job, then that's a problem. Your energy is too infiltrated into something that doesn't mean that much to you. You're not at work and you're still thinking about it. It's not even a job he likes all that much, but he's always there which means there isn't enough balance of personal and professional time. Most of his days are spent at his job. This is not entirely his fault as that's the way the current break-your-back mentality mindset of human physical life is at this time.

Find meaningful work at a place that excites you. Consider the steps that you can start to take today to change this. Imagine how many years you can endure in your current state before your spirit is permanently crushed. This is where faith can help lift you back up to keep going. If you don't have any faith, then it can make the long hike upwards feel like a lifetime.

Most people never have the luxury of ever reaching their dream goals in life. They may feel stuck in a job that is not their dream job, but it pays the bills in a world that is forever ripe with unemployment. Be thankful and grateful you have a job that helps pay the bills while doing your best to continue looking at other options. Maybe the odds are against you, but you'll never know unless you try and increase your chances of succeeding by participating.

Even if you obtain the job of your dreams, there will still be imperfections and issues that arise that need to be dealt with and addressed. The most successful highly paid business super stars are not without issues they have to oversee and resolve. You may not be in your dream job, but make the most of it and use it to your advantage to gain additional experience you did not have before you took the job. The longer you're at a company, then the better that looks on your resume.

To one extent, it is easier to find a job when you have a job. This is because you're not stressed out over looking for a job that you'll accept any position offered to you. When you have a steady paycheck coming in, then the burdens to look for another better job are lifted. You can take your time looking for that improved job while you have income coming in. You're more relaxed about the job hunting scenario you've decided to undertake. In the meantime, you're building additional work experience. The flip negative side to that is you may stay at a job you despise fearful of accepting other job offers wondering if it will end up being worse than the one you have now. This is a minor challenge that could go on in your inner mental debate.

With all of your endeavors think the words, *"I am ferociously fearless!"*

Stand in your awesome power, hone in on what you desire with laser sharp focus, and dive right on in and seize it. When you are one with God, you are never alone, and there is nothing you cannot accomplish.

CHAPTER FOURTEEN

Partake In Work That Pleases

*I*f you don't have dreams you'd like to accomplish while here, then what are you here for? Is it to sit around all day watching daytime television that sucks the intelligence and life force right out of you? Is it to work at a mundane job that makes you miserable? What kind of work would make you happy to do? What action steps can you take to achieve that dream? Sometimes you will have to start from scratch and at the bottom, but if it's work you enjoy doing, then you would be willing to do it for free if you have all the time and money in the world. It is what brings you joy.

Follow your soul's ultimate purpose while ensuring your physical survival. None of that has anything to do with the Devil, unless of course you're going about it through underhanded deceptive means.

If you work hard enough with persistence, passion, and optimism, then you can achieve abundance. If you don't try, then you won't have a shot. Someone wins an award on stage and they give a raving inspiring speech telling viewers they too can be where they are, as they were once living the hard life you were. Now the person longing for positive change feels inspired by that speech.

The person that is on that stage worked extra hard to get where they are. They were getting up at the crack of dawn to go to auditions in hopes of being cast in the right movie that can get them noticed. They were not an overnight success. It might seem there are overnight successes where someone put a product out there that shoots them to the top of the map. If you view their life history you'll see that it took them a long time to get there. They were forever working hard in the area of their interest, then they got lucky by putting something out that seemed to catch universal attention.

Entertainer musicians Shania Twain and Alanis Morissette both had put an album or two out at the start of their music careers that did nothing or wasn't successful. They continued at their passion and ended up producing an album that shot to #1 This propelled them into massive worldwide success. Shania Twain's "*The Woman in Me*", and Alanis Morissette's "*Jagged Little Pill*" were those albums respectively.

Many think of those albums as their first release, but they had other works before that which never had much lift off. Before that point they were working hard at their craft and enjoying their work with minimal to no success, then they got lucky. They fueled fire into their creative endeavors producing work they loved for the joy of it, then they were skyrocketed to worldwide long term success at a later date.

Napoleon Hill, the author of one of the top popular law of attraction books, "*Think and Grow Rich*" was reportedly not rich when he wrote that book. The irony is that he was in the middle of struggle, yet ended up writing a book about being rich and obtaining financial abundance long before he received those riches by writing that book. Through the laws of attraction he made his dreams come true by writing about the topic.

You could be exceptionally great at what you do, but just because no one is buying your products doesn't mean you're no good at what you do. It just means that there weren't the right marketing techniques to get it in front of the right people to purchase your products. Your work can also be far ahead of its time. A great many successful artists rose to prominence long after they passed on when the masses finally realized there was something great there. They just hadn't heard of it at the time it originally came out.

You could be putting in the hard work, you have

a great product, you have marketed your products and yourself, you've been on social media, yet you continue to struggle and lose interest and faith that you'll get that lucky break. This doesn't mean you're doing anything wrong. Having that one lucky break can get you in the door, but staying in the door is your talent and hard work. You want to avoid beating yourself up when something like this happens. When it does, do not falter, but rise up stronger and keep forging on! Continue to do your work and believe one day a breakthrough will happen. If you genuinely and truly enjoy your work, then it doesn't feel like work. You'll do it regardless if anyone buys it or not.

You watch motivational teachers charging a ton of money to attend their seminars about getting rich and attracting in abundance. They do really well at that job because it's currently a hot market to tap into at the moment. If you've got a great personality that shines on camera, then you too can put yourself on camera and monetize it in videos on places like *You Tube,* or on podcasts on *iTunes* and survive making money that way. It may be unlikely that this trend will end anytime soon since obtaining riches has been exotic and enticing since long before Christ.

The Secret book and film rose to popularity because journalist host Oprah Winfrey brought it to light on her show when it ran. When she brought anything to light on her show, then it became a sure fire hit. Had she not done that, no one would've bothered with it. The mass marketing preceding that made it an even bigger success. It was packaged and put together in a way that is attractive to a consumer.

This doesn't mean that the *Secret* works or doesn't work. There are consumers on both sides of the fence believing it does with others believing it doesn't. How many times have you bought a product that looked good online, only to receive it and find that the contraption doesn't work as great as it did online?

Oprah believes in this positive thinking. She also worked hard and took jobs to forge on towards making her passion and dreams come true. It was more than just positive thinking, but the action and hard work on top of that.

There are flaws with the laws of attracting in abundance, as there are flaws with many concepts that work for some people. Sometimes concepts work for some people and other times they don't. It doesn't mean that those it didn't work for didn't do it right. It just means it didn't work for them.

When you imagine and visualize that something you want is going to take place with great veracity, and you couple that with action, then you will be that much closer to bringing in what you desire. I have had those situations come to light in a big way all throughout the course of my life. If it didn't, then I wouldn't bother teaching and discussing this abundance and law of attraction business. Because it has worked for me time and again, I can back it up.

Sometimes you have to participate in jobs that might not necessarily be your passion, but in essence you're gaining training and skills that will be applied towards your true passion. Sometimes that's not initially seen as what's happening until later.

It takes a warrior like effort to not allow anything to kill off your life force and prevent you from working on your passion and life purpose. There are a great many success stories out there throughout history. They included people who were once struggling and wondering if they'd ever break free, but they kept working hard on what they desired on the side during their down time. Eventually they transitioned out of that and into what they love.

Keep forging on ahead fearlessly and making a personal pact to contribute a little bit of what you love towards your lifelong goals each day for a minimum of thirty minutes to an hour. Whether that hour is used to read and research on your areas of interest, or to devote something positive towards what will ultimately be your life purpose income, such as creating a website, a social media page, postcards, etc. Putting in a tiny bit of time each day and week is better than putting in no time.

Be independent and self-sufficient. Working seventy hours a week doesn't mean you're a hard worker. It just means you're not great at time management. It's a world of workaholics plugging away at meaningless tasks that rarely amount to much. This carries into all aspects of your life, but is primarily beneficial for those in leadership or boss superior positions.

When spreading yourself too thin, you want to ensure to be extra careful about what you're putting into your body. You might complain you're too tired or don't have enough time or energy to contribute up to an hour a day into what could potentially be your full-time job. This is a dilemma and a block for you, but if this is work you truly love, then it doesn't feel like work. It's something you enjoy doing, so working on it is rarely a problem. When someone cheerfully wants to do something, they will do it no matter how tired they are. In fact, putting in work on your passion and love gives you a positive lift, an energy boost, and raises your vibration. All of which are ingredients in that recipe for attracting in positive circumstances, energy, and abundance.

CHAPTER FIFTEEN

*Divine Wisdom
on the Laws of Attracting Abundance*

Raising your vibration is a crucial element in giving you greater energy and a brighter mood. This encourages you to make the time to contribute towards what you love. Even after a long day at work at your day job, when you have more energy, then that's energy to help push you to contribute towards work that you love.

The reason you might be exhausted at the end of each day is not always because work is so tough at your day job, but it's because this job does not excite you on any level. When you experience excitement, then the feel good chemical dopamine is released into your system. When you despise what you do, then this depletes the dopamine, which sucks the life force energy right out of you.

When I'm doing what I love, then the energy keeps going for hours where I don't want to stop. It's a perpetual rushed excited high, because I'm doing what I love that it doesn't feel like work. It's fun and I'm getting paid for it too! On top of that, I'm being extra careful with what I put in my body and system. You know that if you have a glass of wine or a beer in the middle of the day, then you're unlikely to put in any work into what you love.

Keeping your energy high and motivated on those days that you want to work on your life purpose requires taking care of all aspects of your body, mind, and soul. When you believe that great things will happen for you, then great things will happen! The ingredients in this recipe include having a positive attitude, strong faith, asking for help in prayer, and taking action. Like the Journey song title says, "Don't Stop Believing."

For some successful people, there will come that point when the floodgates of abundance open and it soars wonderfully into your world. Some personalities will allow the ego to rise convincing you to panic and worry that it's a fluke and will be taken away from you soon enough. Some form of worry could be considered understandable, but don't let it consume and drown you. Quickly move away from that way of thinking and receive the blessings with a positive spirit.

Whenever I started a new film production for

the film studios, people were unaware that I had the occasional minor fear. I would worry the first few days that I might get fired. I would go into a serious meditation exercise the night before my first day on the job and be prepared to dive on in and hit the ground running. The minor fear or worry was so miniscule though that it didn't dominate, but was rather a fleeting thought that peeked its face in, then blew away just as quickly.

After the first number of days on the gig, the fears would subside, as I'd fall into the groove of the job. Employers would later comment they were surprised to hear that I'd have doubts in the beginning, because it never showed. It would pop in for thirty seconds, then pop right out as I'd re-align, let it go, and just do the best job I can do.

It's a wonderful and awesome thing when circumstances start flowing positively. You think, "Wow, I can't believe how great this is. I hope it doesn't go away and I don't lose it."

Don't doubt, just accept, and enjoy the wave of excitement and optimism. Allow any roadblocks in your life to fall away as you move into smooth calm waters up ahead.

Get optimistic, have faith, and trust in God and your Spirit team. When you're worried about something, then ask and pray for intervention to remove those worries. Make this prayer request daily if the worry continues. Don't give up or try to do it yourself, but turn your worries into prayer, since that's what can help lift the burdens that negative thoughts and feelings can produce.

Prayer is intended to help you move away from

worry and fear. You invalidate a prayer when you continue to worry afterwards. The worry tells Spirit that you don't trust their intervention and assistance and so you will continue to worry as a backup plan in case God doesn't come through. When you receive repeated nudges after the prayer to take action on something, then take action.

When circumstances become too great, then take some time out in quiet meditation or contemplation. Create a sanctuary ambiance at home or in your room. Disconnect from people and technology for several hours or even the day, and spend that time conversing with God, a higher power, and the universe. Go on a day or weekend trip with a positive optimistic friend, or by yourself if you find that more beneficial.

Let go of feelings of resentment and jealousy about other people who seem to be more successful than you are at this point. This success may be in career, love, or life in general. You find yourself saying things like, "Why does she have him for a boyfriend? I'm so much better than she is, I don't get it."

Or, "I should be way more successful than they are. I work harder and I'm smarter."

You want to avoid falling into envy energy, because that will ensure you stay single or will never be successful. It's understandable to a point that you are feeling frustrated because you are just as deserving as anyone else of blessings. Resentment builds and overpowers you crushing your soul in the process.

The flipside is if you are financially successful,

then don't feel guilty about making money in general, or making more money than others. Money is energy, so when you're being paid for services you provide, then that is an exchange of energy. Feel no guilt about making money or how you choose to spend it. You are worthy of making money for any work you do. Don't apologize for being blessed.

Avoid resentment, jealousy, worry, or fear associated with money. Visualize the awesome circumstances you'd be able to partake in due to making enough money. Imagine how many people's lives you'd be able to change and help positively.

Your imagination is a powerful divine instrument of God, so use it to your advantage. You're already spending the day thinking, perhaps thinking about useless chores and tasks, but how about thinking about something good. Pay attention to those ideas that enter your mind. A great deal of it is coming from above. Look at the great music, books, art, and movies over the course of history that started out with one person's idea and rapidly expanded to the point where there is a 600-man crew filming it into a visual story. It's awesome what people have been able to create.

The angels don't want to see someone destined for greatness partaking in activities that kill off their life force. They are not keeping you down and nor are they keeping you in a situation to punish you. There could be various reasons as to why you're in an undesired situation beyond your control. Your guides could be working diligently behind the scenes with aligning circumstances that work in your favor to get you to where you want to be.

Release any vows of poverty you might have made in a past life, regardless if you believe in past lives or not. It won't hurt you to verbally say, "I release all vows of poverty I might have made in this life or any previous ones, in all directions of time."

When you hit a wall or roadblock, or your life isn't where you thought it would be, avoid self-blame and blaming others. Some tend to blame the world for their setbacks. It takes a great deal of mental strength to rise above playing the victim. Level headed professionals don't dwell on mistakes, but have the mindset of finding solutions. It's the same way an inexperienced boss will say, "What did you do!?" An experienced boss will say, "How can we fix this?"

Don't shy away or fear problems or challenges that arise. Take a moment to re-center yourself, then examine the options to fixing the issue. Sometimes a problem will take longer than expected to fix depending on the severity of it, but don't let it stop you or bring you down. Those problems and challenges are what contributes to your soul's growth. Soul growth doesn't happen when things are going amazingly. Accelerated soul growth happens through challenges and difficult times.

Some additional tips and guidance to make note of on your personal road path towards attracting in abundance are changing your attitude. If you want to be successful, then surround yourself with successful people. This isn't just financial success, but it can be professional success, personal success, or soul success. These are the people that are driven, passionate, and hard working. They constantly thrive to achieve greatness on some level.

Every day I wake up, one of the things that sifts through my mind with my team is what can I accomplish today. Because of that attitude I've had since childhood, the majority of my friends are successful in some way. I didn't consciously seek those types of personalities out. By the laws of attraction we were drawn to each other due to this common mutual element we all possessed. My personality has never jived well with the ones that have too much time on their hands, no goals they're working towards, or that spend their days gossiping, are idle, slacking, or desiring some form of constant attention. It's like putting two opposing personalities in the room. If you put a slacker who has never had any drive for anything with a go-getter personality, they're not going to connect that well due to how foreign both personalities are.

The same way you are what you eat, you are who you associate with. Human beings are adaptable and you start to take on certain traits of those people around you often without realizing it. Since this is the case, you want to choose who you surround yourself with wisely.

If you're interested in any form of success, then surround yourself with successfully driven people. Again this is not necessarily that financially hungry businessman, but success on any level that is connected to self-improvement and personal success. In order to attract what you want, you have to first also embody the character traits of what you want and who you want to be.

There are some circumstances, which cannot practically be understood by the human mind. Navigate through life with an open mind and consciousness over what is unseen.

Have no fear or doubts in believing in Heaven, God, Jesus, and your Spirit team. Believe that you are watched over and are not being ignored, even on those days when you just want to throw in the towel and permanently give up. Don't give up because there is a reason you are here. Spirit can see the good up ahead, even when you feel like this is it.

The world spins around, circumstances change, friendships come and go, some stay, some leave, people pass on, life goes on for the soul. Study and read up on success stories that you can do it! Don't feel resentment or jealousy over someone else's work, but feel inspired and motivated by it instead. It's to help you feel those things so that you can believe that yes you can do it too.

When one thinks of success they automatically equate it to money, but success is not always financial or monetary. The utmost form of success is how evolved your soul develops in one lifetime. Since this is the true measure of Spirit's view of success, then you should thrive to push the billionaire mark and into abundance enlightenment. Rise above the world around you and dive deep into the depths of possibilities by working to expand your mind and consciousness. Seek out the vast reservoirs of wisdom, knowledge, and intelligence that the Universe holds. Take that by the reigns and soar full speed ahead by making some great things happen in your life today.

Attracting in Abundance

*Opening the Divine Gates to Inviting in Blessings and Prosperity
Through Body, Mind, and Soul Spirit*

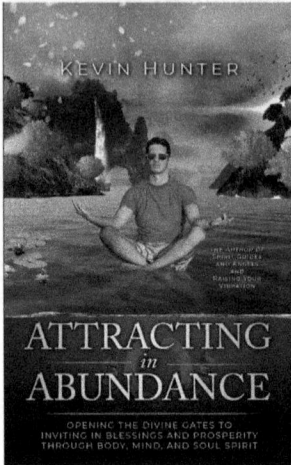

When you hear the word abundance, you may equate it to being blessed with a plentiful overflowing amount of money that equates to a big lottery win. Having enough money to survive comfortably enough on this physical plane is part of obtaining abundance, but it's not the destination and purpose to thrive for. You could work hard to make enough money to the point you are set for life, but that won't necessarily equate to happiness. Achieving a content satisfied state of joy and serenity starts with examining your soul's state and overall well-being. When that's in place, then the rest will follow.

Attracting in Abundance combines practical and spirit wisdom surrounding the nature of abundance. This is something that most everyone can get on board with because all human beings desire physical comforts, blessings, and prosperity, regardless of their personal values and belief systems. *Attracting in Abundance* is broken up into three parts to help move you towards inviting abundance into your life on all levels. "Part One" contains some no-nonsense lectures surrounding the philosophies, concepts, and debates on the laws of attracting in abundance. "Part Two" is the largest of the sections geared towards fine tuning the soul into preparing for abundance. "Part Three" is the final lesson plan to help crack open the gates of abundance with various helpful tidbits, guidance, and messages as well as the blocks that can prevent abundance from coming in.

ALSO BY KEVIN HUNTER

Warrior of Light
Empowering Spirit Wisdom
Darkness of Ego
Realm of the Wise One
Transcending Utopia
Reaching for the Warrior Within
Spirit Guides and Angels
Soul Mates and Twin Flames
Raising Your Vibration
Divine Messages for Humanity
Connecting with the Archangels
Monsters and Angels
The Seven Deadly Sins
Love Party of One
Twin Flame Soul Connections
A Beginner's Guide to the Four Psychic Clair Senses
Attracting in Abundance
Tarot Card Meanings
Abundance Enlightenment
Living for the Weekend
Ignite Your Inner Life Force
Awaken Your Creative Spirit
The Essential Kevin Hunter Collection

The Essential Kevin Hunter Collection
Available in Paperback and E-book

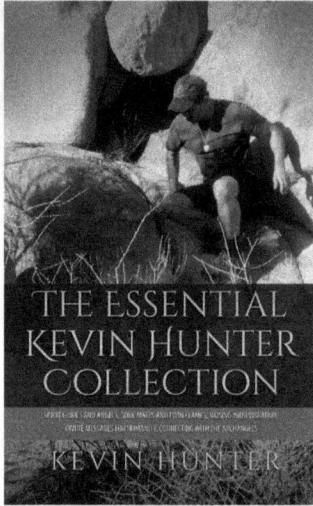

THE ESSENTIAL
KEVIN HUNTER
COLLECTION

Featuring the following books:
Warrior of Light, Empowering Spirit Wisdom, Darkness of Ego,
Spirit Guides and Angels, Soul Mates and Twin Flames, Raising
Your Vibration, Divine Messages for Humanity, and Connecting
with the Archangels.

WARRIOR OF LIGHT
Messages from my Guides and Angels

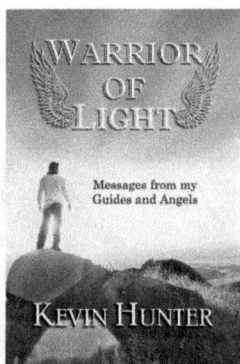

There are legions of angels, spirit guides, and departed loved ones in heaven that watch and guide you on your journey here on Earth. They are around to make your life easier and less stressful. Learn how you can recognize the guidance of your own Spirit team of guides and angels around you. Author, Kevin Hunter, relays heavenly guided messages about getting humanity, the world, and yourself into shape. He delivers the guidance passed onto him by his own Spirit team on how to fine tune your body, soul and raise your vibration. Doing this can help you gain hope and faith in your own life in order to start attracting in more abundance.

EMPOWERING SPIRIT WISDOM
A Warrior of Light's Guide on Love, Career and the Spirit World

Kevin Hunter relays heavenly, guided messages for everyday life concerns with his book, *Empowering Spirit Wisdom*. Some of the topics covered are your soul, spirit and the power of the light, laws of attraction, finding meaningful work, transforming your professional and personal life, navigating through the various stages of dating and love relationships, as well as other practical affirmations and messages from the Archangels. Kevin Hunter passes on the sensible wisdom given to him by his own Spirit team in this inspirational book.

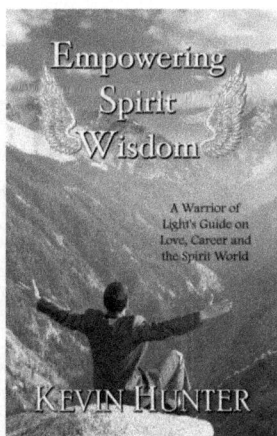

DARKNESS OF EGO

In *Darkness of Ego*, author Kevin Hunter infuses some of the guidance, messages, and wisdom he's received from his Spirit team surrounding all things ego related. The ego is one of the most damaging culprits in human life. Therefore, it is essential to understand the nature of the beast in order to navigate gracefully out of it when it spins out of control. Some of the topics covered in *Darkness of Ego* are humanity's destruction, mass hysteria, karmic debt, and the power of the mind, heaven's gate, the ego's war on love and relationships, and much more.

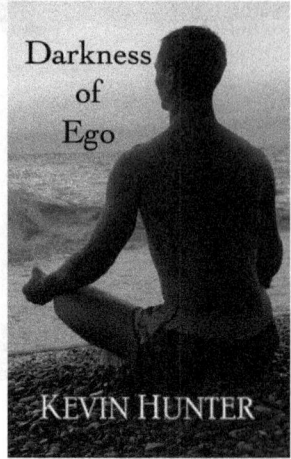

REACHING FOR THE WARRIOR WITHIN

Reaching for the Warrior Within is the author's personal story recounting a volatile childhood. This led him to a path of addictions, anxiety and overindulgence in alcohol, drugs, cigarettes and destructive relationships. As a survival mechanism, he split into many different "selves". He credits turning his life around, not by therapy, but by simultaneously paying attention to the messages he has been receiving from his Spirit team in Heaven since birth.

REALM OF THE WISE ONE

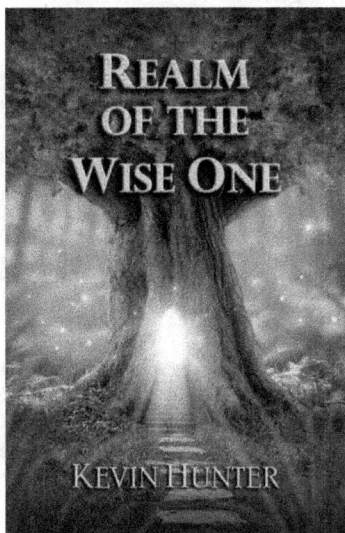

In the Spirit Worlds and the dimensions that exist, reside numerous kingdoms that house a plethora of Spirits that inhabit various forms. One of these tribes is called the Wise Ones, a darker breed in the spirit realm who often chooses to incarnate into a human body one lifetime after another for important purposes.

The *Realm of the Wise One* takes you on a magical journey to the spirit world where the Wise Ones dwell. This is followed with in-depth and detailed information on how to recognize a human soul who has incarnated from the Wise One Realm. Author, Kevin Hunter, is a Wise One who uses the knowledge passed onto him by his Spirit team of Guides and Angels to relay the wisdom surrounding all things Wise One. He discusses the traits, purposes, gifts, roles, and personalities among other things that make up someone who is a Wise One. Wise Ones have come in the guises of teachers, shaman, leaders, hunters, mediums, entertainers and others. *Realm of the Wise One* is an informational guide devoted to the tribe of the Wise Ones, both in human form and on the other side.

TRANSCENDING UTOPIA

Available in Paperback and E-book

Transcending Utopia is packed with practical and spirit knowledge that focuses on enhancing your life through empowering divinely guided spiritual related teachings, inspiration, wisdom, guidance, and messages. The way to accelerate existence on Earth towards Utopia is if every person on the planet resided in their soul's true nature, which is in a state of all love, joy, and peace. The ultimate Nirvana is surpassing that perfection through methods that a limited consciousness could ever dream possible. This is the exceptional glory your soul was born into before the dense turbulence of Earthly life enveloped and suffocated you.

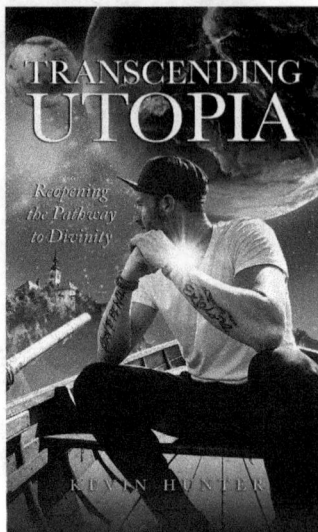

Transcending Utopia is to go beyond your limits and travel outside of the generic mundane materialistic achievement that human beings taught one another to thrive for. A utopian society is where everything is perfectly blissful on all levels according to the sanctified values you were born with. The sensations connected to how flawless everything feels in that moment reveals the authentic perfection you were made from. Utopia is the ideal paradise as imagined in one's dreams that seems to be inaccessible by human standards. It is a state of mind that is possible to reach by adopting broader ways of looking at circumstances while being disciplined about how you conduct your life. You search for a sign of this utopia through external means, only to be consistently left with disappointment. This is because utopia begins and ends inside the spark that burns within your spirit like a pilot light waiting to be ignited.

Living for the Weekend

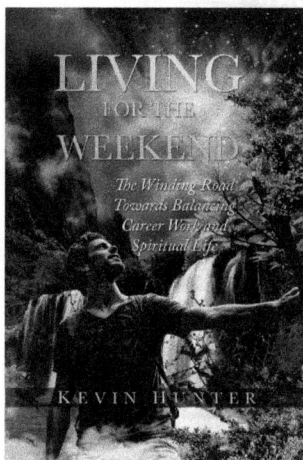

The Winding Road Towards Balancing Career Work and Spiritual Life

Available in Paperback and E-book

Working hard to ensure your bills are paid can leave your soul spiritually starved for soul nourishment. When your ultimate goal is to obtain enough money to be comfortable that you become carried away in that current, then there is little to no room for Divine enrichment.

Many work to survive in jobs they hate because it's the way it is. As a result, they experience and endure all sorts of emotional pain whether it is through depression, sadness, anger, or any other kind of negative stressor. Some silently suffer through this emotional strain gradually killing off their life force. If you don't have a healthy social life and positive fun filled activities and hobbies to balance that burden outside of that, then that could add additional tension. What's it all for if you can't live the life you've always wanted to live? Instead, you spend your days growing forever miserable and broken.

Living for the Weekend examines the pitfalls, struggles, as well as the benefits available in the current modern day working world. This is followed up with spiritual and practical tips, guidance, messages, and discussions on ways to incorporate more balance and enlightenment to a cutthroat material driven world.

MONSTERS
AND ANGELS

An Empath's Guide to Finding Peace in a Technologically Driven World Ripe with Toxic Monsters and Energy Draining Vampires

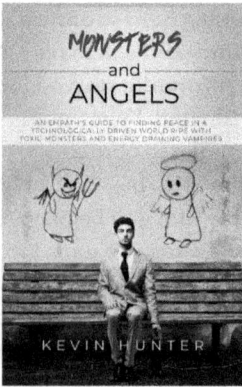

Every person on the planet is capable of being empathic and sensitive, to becoming an energy vampire or toxic monster. No one is exempt from displaying the darker sides of their ego. The easiest and most efficient way to spread any kind of energy is online. Every time you log onto the Internet, there is a larger chance you're going to see something related to the news, media, or gossip areas thrown in front of you, even if you attempt to avoid it as much as possible. You're absorbing everything that your consciousness faces, including the ugly and the wicked, which has its own consequences. This tempestuous energy is tossed into the Universe ultimately creating a flame-throwing battleground inside and around you.

Monsters and Angels discusses how technology, media, and social media have an immense power in distributing both positive and negative influences far and wide. This is about being mindful of what can negatively affect your state of being, and how to counter and avoid that when and wherever possible. This is why it's beneficial to govern yourself, your life, and your surroundings like a strict disciplined executive.

Twin Flame Soul Connections

*Recognizing the Split Apart, the Truths and Myths of Twin Flames,
Soul Love Connections, Soul Mates, and Karmic Relationships*

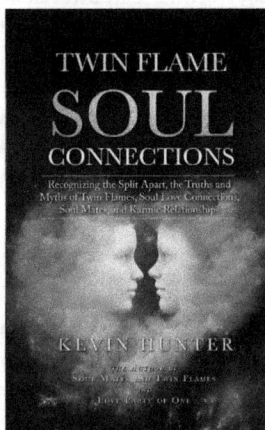

Twin Flames have a shared ongoing sentiment and quest from the moment they're a spark shooting out of God's love that explodes into a blinding white fire that breaks apart causing one to be two, until two become one again, separate and whole, and back around again. Looking into the eyes of your Twin Flame is like looking into the eyes of God, because to know love is to know God.

When one thinks of a Soul Mate or Twin Flame, they might equate it to a passionate romantic relationship where you're making love on a white sandy palm tree lined beach in paradise for the rest of your lives. This beautiful mythological notion has caused great turmoil in others who long for this person that fits the description of a lothario character in a romance novel. It is also an unrealistic and misguided interpretation of the Soul Mate or Twin Flame dynamic.

Twin Flame Soul Connections discusses and lists some of the various myths and truths surrounding the Twin Flames, and how to identify if you've come into contact with your Twin Flame, or if you know someone who has. The ultimate goal is not to find ones Twin Flame, but to awaken ones heart to love, and to work on becoming complete and whole as an individual soul through spiritual self-mastery, life lessons, growth, and raising your consciousness. Your soul's life was born out of love and will die right back into that love.

IGNITE YOUR INNER LIFE FORCE

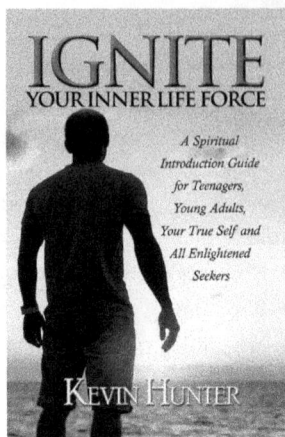

Ignite Your Inner Life Force is an introduction guide for teens, young adults, and anyone seeking answers, messages, and guidance and surrounding spiritual empowerment. This is from understanding what Heaven, the soul, and spiritual beings are to knowing when you are connecting with your Spirit team of Guides and Angels. Some of the topics covered are communicating with Heaven, working with your Spirit team, what your higher self is, your life purpose and soul contract, what the ego is, love and relationships, your vibration energy, shifting your consciousness and thinking for yourself even when you stand alone. This is an in-depth primer manual offering you foundation as you find a higher purpose navigating through your personal journey in today's modern day practical world.

AWAKEN YOUR CREATIVE SPIRIT

Your creative spirit is more than being artistic and getting involved in creativity pursuits, although this is a good part of it. When your creative spirit is activated by a high vibration state of being, then this is the space you create from. You can apply this to your dealings in life, your creative and artistic pursuits, and to having a greater communication line with your Spirit team on the Other Side. *Awaken Your Creative Spirit* is an overview of what it means to have access to Divine assistance and how that plays a part in arousing the muse within you in order to bring your state of mind into a happier space.

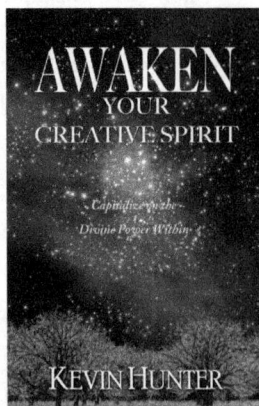

The *Warrior of Light* series of pocket books are available in paperback and E-book called, *Spirit Guides and Angels, Soul Mates and Twin Flames, Divine Messages for Humanity, Raising Your Vibration, Connecting with the Archangels,* and *The Seven Deadly Sins*

TAROT CARD MEANINGS

A Beginner's Guide to the
FOUR PSYCHIC CLAIR SENSES

Learn about the four main psychic clair senses to help you connect with Heaven, the Spirit World, and the Other Side. Take that one step further and use those senses to read the Tarot! *Tarot Card Meanings* is an encyclopedia reference guide that takes the Tarot apprentice reader through each of the 78 Tarot Cards offering the potential general meanings and interpretations that could be applied when conducting a reading, whether it be spiritual, love, general, or work related questions. This is an easy to understand manual for the Tarot novice that is having trouble interpreting cards for themselves, or a Tarot reader who loves the craft and is looking for a refresher or another point of view. The *Four Psychic Clair Senses* focuses on the main channels that Heaven and Spirit communicate with you. *Both books are available in Paperback and E-book wherever books are sold.*

About Kevin Hunter

Kevin Hunter is the metaphysical spiritual author of more than two-dozen spiritually based books that tackle a variety of genres and tend to have a strong male protagonist. The messages and themes he weaves in his work surround Spirit's own communications of love and respect, which he channels and infuses into his writing work.

His spiritually based empowerment books include *Warrior of Light, Empowering Spirit Wisdom, Realm of the Wise One, Reaching for the Warrior Within, Darkness of Ego, Transcending Utopia, Living for the Weekend, Ignite Your Inner Life Force, Awaken Your Creative Spirit,* and *Tarot Card Meanings.* His metaphysical pocket books series include, *Spirit Guides and Angels, Soul Mates and Twin Flames, Raising Your Vibration, Divine Messages for Humanity, Connecting with the Archangels, The Seven Deadly Sins, Four Psychic Clair Senses, Monsters and Angels, Twin Flame Soul Connections, Attracting in Abundance,* and *Abundance Enlightenment.* He is also the author of the dating singles guide *Love Party of One,* the horror/drama, *Paint the Silence,* and the modern day erotic love story, *Jagger's Revolution.*

Kevin started out in the entertainment business in 1996 as the personal development guy to one of Hollywood's most respected talent, Michelle Pfeiffer, for her boutique production company, Via Rosa Productions. She dissolved her company after several years and he made a move into coordinating film productions for the studios on such films as *One Fine Day, A Thousand Acres, The Deep End of the Ocean, Crazy in Alabama, The Perfect Storm, Original Sin, Harry Potter & the Sorcerer's Stone, Dr. Dolittle 2,* and *Carolina.* He considers himself a beach bum born and raised in Southern California. For more information: www.kevin-hunter.com